Jacob's Hip

Jacob's Hip

Finding God
in an Anxious Age

Kerry Walters

ORBIS BOOKS

Maryknoll, New York 10545

Founded in 1970, Orbis Books endeavors to publish works that enlighten the mind, nourish the spirit, and challenge the conscience. The publishing arm of the Maryknoll Fathers and Brothers, Orbis seeks to explore the global dimensions of the Christian faith and mission, to invite dialogue with diverse cultures and religious traditions, and to serve the cause of reconciliation and peace. The books published reflect the views of their authors and do not represent the official position of the Maryknoll Society. To learn more about Maryknoll and Orbis Books, please visit our website at www.maryknoll.org.

Manufactured in the United States of America.
Manuscript editing and typesetting by Joan Weber Laflamme.

Library of Congress Cataloging-in-Publication Data

Walters, Kerry S.
  Jacob's hip : finding God in an anxious age / Kerry Walters.
      p. cm.
Includes bibliographical references.
  ISBN 1-57075-437-3
  1. Spirituality—Catholic Church. I. Title.
    BX2350.65 .W347 2003
    248.8'6—dc21
                                                          2002009840

For Kim and Jonah
Who love me into vulnerability

Contents

⊰ Introduction ⊱

Wrestling with Vulnerability

> *The great challenge is living*
> *our wounds through.*
> —HENRI NOUWEN, *THE INNER VOICE OF LOVE*

A Startling Encounter

This little book might never have been written but for the grandmotherly woman who walked out of church one morning and gave me the finger.

A few days after 9/11, when everyone in the nation was reeling in horror from the terrorist attacks and almost everyone was crying out in rage and grief for swift military retaliation, a few of us in my small town began holding public peace vigils. Laden with two or three signs and a crucifix, we stood for an hour each week on a corner of Main Street to mourn the victims, grieve for their loved ones, and pray that the United States would find a nonviolent way to pursue justice.

When the bombing of Afghanistan began in early October, we decided to hold a marathon vigil, beginning early on a Sunday morning and continuing until dark. It just so happened that three churches with very large and very respectable congregations were situated within a block of our street corner. As church services ended that Sunday morning, most of the departing worshipers passed by us.

We expected our fellow Christians to sympathize with what we were doing. We quickly discovered just how naive that hope was. With only a few exceptions, families dressed in their Sunday best heckled, fathers' faces turned beet red with fury, mothers gustily swore at us as their kids listened in wide-eyed amazement. One older man driving past us actually pulled his well-groomed SUV to a brake-squealing halt, the better to bellow out: "You goddamn assholes! I just got through praying for pricks like you!"

Then, in the midst of this unrelenting verbal assault, I saw her walking toward us: a stately, stylishly dressed woman, seventy or so years old if she was a day. She carried her purse on one arm and a prayer book under the other. Her hair was bluish white. There was a faint smile on her face that suggested compassion and goodwill. I latched onto the sight of her like a wounded soldier fixes his gaze on a sister of mercy. I just *knew* she'd give us a kind word as she passed. When she got abreast of me, I shot her a big grin, inviting her encouragement, asking for her blessing.

She looked at me, she looked at the signs, she looked at the crucifix I was holding. The smile stayed on her face, but it took on a tight, steely quality. Then, staring me right in the eyes, she flipped me off.

I was so stunned I almost dropped the crucifix.

Rage and Panic

I've thought a lot about this encounter, trying to understand why I found it so disturbing. At first I figured that its theater-of-the-absurd incongruity was what threw me. After all, it's not every day that a grandmotherly church lady hoists a middle finger in your direction. But it finally dawned on me that the real source of my disquiet lay elsewhere. I realized that the church lady was just a sign of the blind rage with which most people in this country responded to those who, in the wake of 9/11, sought an alternative to war. And that rage, in turn, spewed forth from a far more ancient wound than the terrorist attacks.

It is not difficult to understand the rage. It was spawned by panic. All of us were scared to death in the days immediately following the terrorist attacks. Nor, after months of periodic national security alerts and ominous assurances from senior political leaders that more terrorist assaults are inevitable, has the fear really disappeared. We're still jittery. A few seconds of dead air on the radio can send our hearts thumping. Too many jet streaks in the sky make us want to rush into the house and flip on CNN. These days, no one hears low rumbling thunder without wondering, if only for a second, if it is more than just thunder. Always, somewhere in the back of our minds, we're waiting for the other shoe to drop. If the unthinkable happened once, it can happen again.

Part of the reason for this pervasive anxiety is the sense that more than just our personal well-being is in jeopardy. Both our national frontier and our economic and cultural ethos were violated on 9/11, and these broader assaults have profoundly shaken us. As one commentator perceptively put it, the attacks

> struck at the very nerve center of American identity. The World Trade Center and the Pentagon were not simply large buildings previously deemed safe from attack; they were the preeminent symbols of Western capitalism and military might. . . . These buildings were the shadows or projections of archetypal objects: the terrorists had succeeded in attacking America and Western

civilization not on the surface but at a deeper,
much more primal level.[1]

Given all this, it is understandable why many Americans
were outraged by post-9/11 pleas for peace. These sorts of
calls grated on the circle-the-wagon mindset that sprang up:
extreme threats to safety demand swift and merciless response, not dialogue; the only way to protect yourself is to
come out with guns blazing—anything else is suicidal; arm the
torpedoes and shirkers be damned! Either you're with us or
you're against us.

So my church lady's cold fury was born of fear. That much
seems pretty obvious. But what isn't so clear is the reason for
its intensity. After all, public support for military retaliation was
in the mid-ninetieth percentile in the weeks following 9/11.
When weighed against those astoundingly high percentages,
the few dissenting voices scattered across the country were
surely too insignificant to take as serious threats to national
security. Why would a lion work itself into a rage over a gnat?
Yet it did, as evidenced by the church people's attitude that
October morning in my hometown as well as in scores of
other hometowns throughout the nation. The dispropor-
tionality of response to provocation is bewildering.

The Deeper Fear

One of modern psychology's insights is that the causes of
human behavior are often hidden from consciousness. If we
emotionally overreact to a situation, chances are good that
what's *really* yanking our chain is the stirred-up memory of a
past wound or trauma. It happens all the time. When we
explode in anger at a spouse or co-worker, for example, it
could be that we're really yelling at the overbearing mother or

indifferent father of our childhood. Moreover, we continue reacting in this unconsciously backward-looking manner until we steel ourselves to face our old wounds, bring them up to the surface, and offer them an opportunity to air and heal.

I believe that the disproportionately intense rage of my church lady points to a longstanding spiritual wound that all of us share, a wound whose carefully suppressed pain was traumatically aroused on 9/11. The resurfacing of this old ache is the root cause of the rage.

The wound I'm referring to is the primordial and utterly threatening suspicion that life is unfixably unpredictable and unstable, that each individual must wage continuous battle against deadly dangers, and that each of us loses in the end anyway. In our deepest heart, we know ourselves to be the most vulnerable of creatures, prey to every germ or drop in the temperature or neighbor's bad mood that crosses our path. Life is as fragile as gossamer, and our chthonic aware-ness of this dismal but ultimately inescapable fact haunts our days and nights.

If shoved in our face, the unhappy truth about our essential vulnerability would send most of us reeling in panic and despair. So we burn a great deal of psychological fuel trying to deny it. Our culture collaborates in the great deception by teaching us how to scoop out safety zones and erect security barriers for ourselves. The more powerful you are, society tells us, the more invulnerable you are, and power comes with wealth, prestige, knowledge, influence, good looks, and so on.

When an event occurs that challenges our carefully con-trived illusions of untouchability—particularly when it rocks not just our personal lives but the entire ethos of invulnerabil-ity from which we draw sustenance—the ensuing fear isn't merely a response to the immediate threat. More fundamen-tally, it ignites the old, tamped-down anxiety that slumbers at

the center of our being. The urgency so many feel to obliterate terrorists with bombs and missiles and bullets is fueled by
this underground fear of insecurity. Osama bin Laden's
depredations are occasions for declaring war against vulnerability, the ancient nemesis. It only follows that anyone who
refuses to pull his or her weight in the campaign would incite
rage.

Embracing Insecurity

Smart bombs and bigger defense packages and armed national
guardsmen at airports won't heal our deeper woundedness,
even though they might make us feel safer in the short run.
Unless we resolve to face it squarely, our horror of vulnerability will continue to fester in our spiritual innards. But because
the wound is so painful, the temptation to avoid it by concen-
trating on immediate threats to national and personal security
is overwhelming. We want to believe that all we need to get
back to business as usual is to fix the latest mess and then build
higher and stronger security barriers.

The deeper challenge of 9/11 is to confess our dread of
insecurity and our obsession with safety, and then to ask
ourselves if either really makes any sense. Most of us just
naturally assume that invulnerability is a desirable state. But is
it? What if the unintended consequences of safety zones and
security barriers are isolation, alienation, self-absorption, an
erosion of fellow-feeling, and a ratcheting-up of the very
anxiety we hope to avoid? What if our need to be untouchable
actually does us more harm than good?

These are questions well worth asking, because confronting
our entrenched fear of vulnerability isn't just an exercise in
political or social analysis. First and foremost, it's an occasion
for spiritual scrutiny. This is especially the case for those of us

who are Christians, because our dread of vulnerability is
strikingly inconsistent with our faith. As Martin Smith discom-
fortingly reminds us, "We sin by thinking and acting as if other
forces in the world were actually more powerful than the
creative love of God and thus had to be submitted to on their
own terms."[2]

The gospel tells us, "Be not afraid!" The good news is that
Christ's entry into a precarious world has subverted fear,
freeing his followers from the age-old dread of insecurity.

For the most part, we Christians have assumed we should
be unafraid because we are under Christ's protection and thus
insulated from worldly dangers. But this is false. When we're
told not to be afraid, the implication isn't that God's patronage
somehow makes us invulnerable (the roll call of martyrs tells us
this much), but rather that vulnerability isn't anything that
ought to panic us. Insecurity we will always have with us. The
trick is to accept it—indeed, to *embrace* it—as a necessary
and even welcome part of the human condition. It is only by
balancing on the edge, dancing on the margin, that we
become fully human. This is how Jesus himself lived, and it is
the way he encouraged us to live. When we shy away from his
invitation to vulnerability, we become underground creatures
who give up sunshine and fresh air for the sake of a false
security. We enclose ourselves in subterranean bunkers that
may look impregnable from the outside but are dank and
suffocating on the inside.

Or we become proper churchgoing Christians so haunted
by our fear of Christ's lifestyle that, in times of crisis, we flip
off peaceniks and loudly champion war. We are driven to
terrified despair, timorously concluding that 9/11 forever
changed the world and forgetting, as theologian Stanley
Hauerwas reminds us, that in fact it was A.D. 33 that forever
changed the world.[3]

Storms at Sea

Because times of crisis reopen the old wound and bring its
pain and anguish to the surface, they also offer us the chance
to examine the wound, see it for what it is, and free ourselves
from its power.

The terrorist attacks of 9/11 have pushed us into what is
sometimes called a *limit situation*: a time of material, emo-
tional, and spiritual upheaval that forcibly takes us beyond the
boundaries of normalcy. Limit situations propel us out of a
state of secure and safe equilibrium, of "being well settled,
knowing that life makes sense and that God is well placed in
heaven," into one of painful disorientation where life in all its
rawness bushwhacks and overwhelms us.[4] Everything we
thought permanent and absolutely dependable is shaken;
everything we thought unquestionable is up for grabs. The old
safety zones and security barriers no longer protect us.

Horribly painful as such a time of disorientation and fear
can be, it also offers an opportunity—a *kairos,* as the gospel
writers would have said—for seeing, learning, and growing.
Security barriers block our vision. It's difficult to stretch high
enough to peek out over them. But when they are swept away
in a limit situation, a wide vista of possibility suddenly stretches
before us. At first we may suffer intensely from spiritual
agoraphobia. Underground creatures panic when their bur-
rows collapse and they find themselves under open sky. But if
we can endure the initial shock, we will discover we are made
for open places, despite the fact that we are incredibly vulnerable in them. Open, unprotected places are always risky, but
they're also where God and self-insight and true community
are found. As Ralph Waldo Emerson once wrote, "People
wish to be settled; only as far as they are unsettled is there any
hope for them."[5]

The authors of the Hebrew and Christian scriptures knew this and sometimes used the image of a raging sea storm to get the point across. The reluctant prophet Jonah, who preferred to play it safe and sail to friendly Tarshish rather than obey God's instructions to go to the dangerous city of Nineveh, is overtaken by a great storm, cast overboard by terrified sailors, and ultimately finds redemption in the belly of the beast. The Acts of the Apostles tells how Paul is similarly stretched by his own storm at sea. The ship on which he has booked passage puts out into an unfriendly sea rather than seeking haven in a Cretan port. Beset almost immediately by a gale, the vessel is tossed about for two weeks before finally dragging to shore. Paul's trust in God during this limit situation calms and saves the crew. Without it, they would have panicked and despaired.

In both stories, comments Eugene Peterson, the storm is a symbol of the "unleashed spirit/wind of God. Storm is the environment in which we either lose our lives or are saved; there is no cool, safe ledge on which to perch as spectators."[6]

In the midst of the storm we call life, there is no ship's hold strong enough to keep us in total safety. Nor should we crave one. God's will can be discerned only in the open air—in fear, and hope, and trust.

A Lesson from the Jabbok

Wounds, even those that most bedevil us, can also be blessings. This is, of course, the scandalous message of the cross. But it is also a message prefigured on several occasions in the Hebrew scriptures, with one of the most dramatic tellings being the story of Jacob's nocturnal wrestling match.

Jacob—whose name, appropriately, means "the grabber"— is the patron saint of all who dread vulnerability. He spent

most of his life plotting and scheming and conniving to
become untouchable. Like so many of us today, Jacob panicked at the thought of insecurity and fancied he could protect
himself against it by grabbing as much power as he could lay
his hands on. So, beginning at an early age, he started consolidating his safety zone. First he tricked his rather dim-witted
brother, Esau, out of his birthright; then, for good measure, he
also snatched away Esau's blessing by deceiving their blind
father, Isaac. When Esau finally caught on to what brother
Jacob was up to, he flew into a rage and vowed to kill him on
sight. Jacob, true to character, did the safe thing: he fled,
taking both birthright and blessing with him.

Jacob kept running until he reached the land of Haran,
where he eventually settled with his kinsman Laban, married
Leah and Rachel, and proceeded to strengthen his safety zone
by bilking Laban out of most of his herd. When Laban's sons
discovered that Jacob had swallowed up a sizable portion of
their inheritance, they were as angry with him as Esau had
been years earlier. Once again Jacob decided the safest
strategy was flight—this time back to the land of his birth. So
he collected his flocks, his wives, his children—tokens of
strength and security—and headed home.

Upon reaching the Jabbok River, the boundary of his
homeland, Jacob got word of one more threat to his safety: a
still furious Esau was waiting for him with an army of four
hundred men. So Jacob improvised another security barrier.
He sent his wives and eleven children, along with an enor-
mous gift of livestock, across the Jabbok in the hope that if
Esau's heart wasn't melted by the one, his anger would be
mollified by the other. Then Jacob the anxious, restless
grabber, left all to himself on the safe side of the river, sat
down to wait. The sun set and darkness came.

Suddenly some unseen force hit him in the back. Jacob sprang up and wheeled around to meet his attacker. He assumed it was one of Esau's men come to seek vengeance, but the night was too dark for him to see the mysterious other's face. Besides, he had no time to worry about the stranger's identity. He was in a fight for his life.

For hours the two wrestled. By dawn, each was exhausted, barely able to do more than cling stubbornly to the other. Then the attacker fell back on one final trick: pulling an arm free, he struck Jacob's hip and dislocated it.

But Jacob the grabber, Jacob the clinger, still hung onto his assailant like a bulldog. "Let me go!" the astonished stranger shrieked. "Forget it!" roared Jacob. "I'm sticking to you like glue until I get a blessing!"

And, quite unexpectedly, he got his blessing. The stranger, who some identify as God and others as an angel, there and then miraculously transformed Jacob the grabber into Israel, the man "through whom God shows his strength." But the blessing carried a price: Jacob walked with a limp the rest of his days.

What Jacob learned that terrible night on the Jabbok is what we're being called to learn for ourselves today: that wounds, painful as they are, can also bring blessings—that, indeed, the two are frequently identical. What Jacob learned is the great mystery that the cross taught later generations: insecurity, vulnerability, living and dying on the margins, out on the open, unprotected plains, are all opportunities for blessings if we but allow them to speak to our heart and transform us. As one commentator recently put it, "Out of weakness comes strength; out of powerlessness comes power; out of death comes resurrection, life. This is part of the radical witness that Jesus places before us: God's foolishness is wiser than human wisdom and God's weakness stronger than human strength."[7]

We too should stick like glue to the pain and anxiety we feel in the wake of 9/11 until we receive a blessing from it. Like our ancestor Jacob, we must come to realize that limping isn't the worst thing in the world. In fact, it's a reasonable price to pay if it purchases our way across the Jabbok River. Honestly facing the deeper wound re-opened by 9/11 won't make us fearless. We will remain, always, vulnerable creatures. But it *will* enable us to work through our anxiety so that we can better understand and live with it.

This little book is an invitation to begin the process. In Chapter 1, we will examine more closely the vulnerability—or, to borrow a word from Dorothy Day, the "precarity"—of the human condition, and see why in fact it is a great spiritual blessing that ought to be embraced rather than deplored. Chapter 2 explores the way our view of the world is transfigured when we embrace precarity. Chapter 3 argues that genuine community is possible only when we accept our common precarity. And Chapter 4 shows that an acceptance of precarity socially and politically implies fidelity to the "downward" path of reconciliation and peace rather than the "upward" path of military and economic might.

❧ 1 ❧

Beyond Barriers

*Jesus is ground zero, that
totally empty being who
radiates God.*

—John Dear, *Peace behind Bars*

Security Systems

In addition to making us all terribly self-conscious about sex,
that great iconoclast Sigmund Freud further eroded our sense
of well-being by insisting that belief in God is a fear-inspired
neurosis.

We live, says Freud, in a dangerous world. Natural events
and other people threaten us, and death is around every
corner. A handful of hardy folk are able to cope with the
anxiety all this typically inspires, but the vast majority of us
aren't. So, unable to withstand life's cold winds without some
kind of security blanket, we fool ourselves into believing that
an all-powerful god is protectively watching over us. But this,
says Freud, is a pathetic delusion spawned by wishful thinking.
It is a predictable defense strategy, but it is also a neurotic
confusion of illusion and reality.[1]

One can disagree with Freud's atheism and still appreciate
his claim that most of us are frightened of the world in which
we live and that this terror necessarily affects our spirituality.

In fact, fear could well be the most primal human emotion. It certainly seems one of the most ubiquitous. The pelvic thrust at birth that up-ends us into an alien world traumatizes and disorients us, the prospect of plunging into inky darkness at life's terminus fills us with dread, and the million-and-one threats to our well-being that lurk between entrance and exit leave us jittery and anxious. As philosopher Richard Geldard puts it,

> At the most basic level of our existence, we react with fear to every apparent threat from our environment. Our lowest instinct—fight or flight—stimulates the creation of a stock of games and masks in order to protect, deflect, justify, and escape from whatever appears to threaten us. Gradually, these deceptions sheath us in a protective armor to allow us to remain somewhere between the extremes of complete escape (flight) or inhuman violence (fight). The habit of illusion-building at this low level of experience grows to encompass higher levels of experience. By the time we are adults we have clothed ourselves in such elaborate illusions that the task of stripping them away becomes in itself an object of great fear.[2]

Fear ultimately stems from this primordial awareness of our own vulnerability. Significantly, the word *fear* can be traced back to an Old Saxon term that means "ambush" or "sudden calamity." We sense, even if we often refuse to utter, the fragile contingency of our existence, trembling at how easily a flood can break our dams, a burglar steal our possessions, or an invisible microbe take our life. So we frantically seek to protect ourselves from our own vulnerability. Feeling impotent and weak, we struggle mightily to compensate, to acquire through hard work or cunning the protective power denied us at birth. As Michael Ramsey observes, "The human race is afraid and its fears are about power—about having it or not having it. Those who have it are frightened that they may be going to lose it. Those who do not have it are frightened of those with it."[3]

The safety zones and security barriers by which we hope to protect and empower ourselves take many forms. Perhaps the most common one is material ownership. We pad our frailty with the artificial biceps of money and property. Wealth and possessions are buffers against threats from the outside. They protectively encrust our soft underbellies with hard jewels and coins. Why was the rich young man of scripture reluctant to give up his wealth? Because he was addicted to the pleasures it purchased? Perhaps that was part of it. But a more likely explanation is his anxiety that the loss of his wealth would expose him to a ravenous world. Money makes us untouchable. Money is power.

We also try to protect ourselves by using people. This strategy transforms humans into security barriers. We attach ourselves to powerful individuals or groups with the desperate urgency of a playground weakling seeking a protective upperclassman. We scramble to be part of the in-crowd, the movers-and-shakers, the trend-setters and go-getters. This is a special temptation for an adolescent first coming to grips with the anxieties of life, but its allure continues long afterward as well. The right business partners, the right political party, the right neighborhood, the right social club, the right friends, the right congregation: these are all safety zones that make us feel more powerful than we really are. In numbers is strength and power.

Another type of security barrier often overlooked but just as crucial to our sense of empowerment is the conceptual and moral way we look at the world around us. None of us is a pure empiricist. We necessarily read our experiences through certain interpretive lenses, and one of the psychological functions of these interpretations is to help us cope with a frightening world. We re-create our world by feeding experience into non-threatening conceptual frameworks. No matter that these frameworks for the most part are binary: First World *vs.* Third World, anglo *vs.* colored, smart *vs.* dumb, handsome *vs.* homely, male *vs.* female, adult *vs.* child, mine *vs.* yours. The point is that they draw sharp conceptual lines in the sand that circumscribe where it is safe for us to be. Knowledge, Francis Bacon assured us, is power.

All this leads us back, as Freud recognized it must, to our understanding of God. How could it not? If we're as anxious about vulnerability in everyday life as we seem to be, forever scurrying to get behind one security barrier or the other, then surely our horror of being ambushed must influence our spiritual life as well.

And so it does. Many of us who consider ourselves Christian embrace precisely the concept of God that Freud decried: a cosmic Big Daddy fiercely protective of his kids. The only god we deem worthy of our worship (that is, the only god who can give us the safety we crave) is an all-powerful potentate who brooks no challenge to his (of course it would be *his*) authority. This god is the ultimate security barrier, the utterly impregnable safety zone, the fail-safe defense perimeter shielding us from a hostile world. So long as we remain loyal to him, we can invoke his protection. He will armor our frailty and gird our underbelly. God is power, power is strength, and strength is safety.

Granted, few Christians apart from an occasional evangelical zealot explicitly describe God in these terms. But the sentiment is there, rippling through our petitionary pleas for protection from illness, betrayal, financial hardship, or death, our sometimes disturbingly militant icons of Christ or spear-wielding archangels, and our psalms and hymns that proclaim God a mighty fortress. Despite all our sweetly pious talk about Jesus meek and mild or our sentimental attachment to humble saints like Francis of Assisi, the God for whom most of us truly yearn is the safety-zone God—not, mind you, because we're hypocrites, but because we're so very frightened of our own vulnerability.

The upshot, as Freud saw, is that we tend to gravitate toward a spirituality of security. The degree to which our lives are spiritually sound comes to be measured by how safe and anxiety-free we feel. As Lucien Richard insightfully notes, "The contemporary [spiritual] climate is therapeutic. People identify personal salvation with the feeling of personal well-being, personal health, and the psychic security they crave."[4] Having a good relationship with God means that I stand on solid rather than shifting ground, that I am encased in a divine bubble that protectively isolates me from an infectious world (Christians, remember, are "in" but not "of" the world). My existence is no longer fragile because the divine "godfather" has made me an offer I can't refuse. It follows that my own personal holiness can be gauged by how powerful—that is, untouchable—I am in the midst of a dangerous and unpredictable world. Power is a sign of God's favor.

The claim that much of what passes for Christian spirituality these days is a way of coping with our deepest anxiety may be hard to swallow. But how else to account for the extraordinary appeal and commercial success of pop spirituality books that promise faithful Christians big payoffs in this life? Take, for example, Bruce Wilkinson's recent *The Prayer of Jabez*. This slim volume, which has sold hundreds of thousands of copies in addition to spinning off a lucrative product line that includes Jabez journals, Jabez devotionals, Jabez Bible studies, Jabez teen guides, and leather-bound gift edition Jabezes, promises that fidelity to the heavenly godfather will bring "miraculous power in your life *now*."[5] To his credit, Wilkinson occasionally cautions readers that "miraculous power" probably ought to be thought of in supernatural rather than material terms. But he just can't make himself stick to that message very long. In a chapter entitled "Living Large for God," he more typically writes this:

> If Jabez had worked on Wall Street, he might
> have prayed, "Lord, increase the value of my
> investment portfolios." When I talk to presidents
> of companies, I often talk to them about this
> particular mind-set. When Christian executives
> ask me, "Is it right for me to ask God for more
> business?" my response is "Absolutely!" If you're
> doing your business God's way, it's not only right
> to ask for more, but He is waiting for you to ask.[6]

One could scarcely ask for a crisper snapshot of a spirituality of safety. Whatever we do that makes us less vulnerable is pleasing to God because God *wants* us to be safe and secure.

The fly in the ointment is that Freud was right when he nailed all this as wishful thinking. We're called to be Christians, not Jabezites. The Christian God isn't a celestial Don Corleone, the Christian life isn't one of comfortable invulnerability, Jesus didn't come to build security barriers. On the contrary, Jesus' entire ministry was about daring to smash through them. Jesus was the guy, after all, who rattled the play-it-safe Pharisees by breaking the Sabbath, ignoring dietary laws, hanging around with whores, taxmen, and demoniacs, and teeter-tottering on the margin of normalcy—and, moreover, doing it all joyfully, without anxiety for the morrow. Jesus was the teacher who admonished us to give up all our possessions—material as well as spiritual—and embrace poverty. It was Jesus who told us that to be spiritually poor—to be vulnerable in the most harrowing sense of the word—is to live in a state of great blessedness. As John Ferguson reminds us, "Both the Sermon on the Mount and the Sermon on the Plain teach us that we are not to be obsessed with security."[7]

Jesus actually lived his words; even more to the point, he died them. The cross is a symbol of the new message he brought to humankind: God is not only all-powerful, God is also all-powerless. God is love, and love is powerful enough to create a cosmos but vulnerable enough to suffer and die for the beloved's sake. To love is risky business, and to love supremely is to put oneself at supreme risk.

For the Christian, God isn't a place of unassailable security, a divine fallout shelter. God, as John Dear says, is ground zero. God is the bull's-eye in the target. God is that place of radical vulnerability on the other side of the fortress wall.

Cracks in the Bunker

A spirituality based on the fearful need for safety turns out not to be bombproof after all. Wishful thinking is destructive in the long run. To substitute what we want to be the case with what actually is may provide some comforting insulation for a while, but eventually the real world crashes in on our dream land. Reality, C. S. Lewis once said, is the great iconoclast.[8] Sooner or later, it smashes our idols and grinds up our fancies. So the

safety spirituality in which we seek haven is actually built on
sand. With time and tide, it collapses and sweeps us away.

In all honesty, it provides small comfort even before that
dreadful day arrives. The irony of safety spiritualities is that
they actually tend to elevate rather than diminish our anxiety
level. Safety spiritualities, keep in mind, are strategies to tamp
down our deep-seated dread of vulnerability. As such, they
become one of those "possessions" we desperately hope will
empower us. But a nearly inevitable result of depending so
much on possessions is that we are chronically worried about
losing them. Someone might take them away from us, or we
might lose them through sheer bad luck. So we wind up
constantly fretting and fuming about how to protect the very
possessions that are supposed to be protecting us. The
consequence, as John Dear reminds us, is that our efforts to
attain security only shove us into the very danger zones we
hoped to avoid:

> Our First World culture socializes us to cling to
> our possessions. Through fear, insecurity, and
> faithlessness, we accumulate a wide variety of
> paraphernalia. We carry on our shoulders a life-
> time supply of material goods, as well as anger,
> jealousy, bitterness, and violence. These weights
> prevent us from coming before God as we really
> are—vulnerable, ordinary, human beings.[9]

The tragedy is that it is not merely our material goods that
get between us and God. Our spiritual ones do too, if we
measure them in terms of how safe we think they can make
us. Embracing a safety spirituality guarantees that we will
begin to think of God as an insurance agent. So long as we
keep up with our quarterly payments, the policy remains

intact. But if we are ever late in getting our check in the mail, we can be canceled. Even worse, we can be canceled just because the insurer decides for whatever reason that we have become a bad risk. The insurance doesn't alleviate our anxiety. It only gives us something else to worry about.

A Spirituality on the Edge

John Dear says we must come before God as we really are, and that means in all our vulnerable nakedness. To do that, we must embrace a spirituality that frees us to live with our frailty. The heart of that spirituality isn't safety and security. Instead, it is what Dorothy Day called "precarity."

In the minds of most, precarity (or *precariousness*) is a bleak state of uncertainty and danger. The word connotes instability, poverty, marginalization, the absence of a safety net. A precarious economy, a precarious state of health, a precarious relationship: each of these spells trouble. We fear precarity because precarity is vulnerability. Yet, counter-intuitively, Day claims that precarity is a grace for which we ought to pray. "We usually get what we pray for," she says, "and maybe we are afraid to pray for it [precarity]. And yet I am convinced that it is the grace we most need in this age of crisis, this time when expenditures reach into the billions to defend 'our American way of life.'"[10]

We ought to keep in mind that precarity doesn't simply mean "uncertainty." It also suggests radical dependence: the Latin *precarious* is the state of being dependent on another's will, being upheld or sustained by another's force. So a spirituality centered on precarity acknowledges the radical uncertainty or contingency of human existence *and* our utter dependence on God. But the dependence here is quite differ-ent from the kind found in safety spiritualities. The God who upholds us mustn't be thought of as the all-powerful boss of a celestial protection racket. Instead, the God who sustains us *shares* our precarity. God is right there on the margins with us, and it is precisely this shared vulnerability that upholds us.

One way of getting a handle on the full meaning of precarity is to translate it into the more familiar scriptural phrase "spiritual poverty." Jesus commends spiritual poverty in his Sermon on the Mount (Mt 5:3), giving it pride of place among the beatitudes. The implication is that the other blessings are somehow subordinate or flow from this first one. Unless a person has cultivated spiritual poverty, mercy and meekness and a hunger for justice and peace are hard to come by.

Many of us tend to think that what Jesus means by spiritual poverty is a turn-the-other-cheek kind of passivity. But in fact this is too timid an interpretation. Jesus' understanding of poverty is much more subversive than that. If we look at the Greek, we discover just how dark and frightening—but also liberating—his words actually are.

The expression translated as "the poor in spirit" is *ptochoi tou pneumati. Ptochos* is one of two words for "poverty" found in scripture, and it has a terrible meaning. To be in a state of *ptoches* isn't simply to be materially poor in the sense of living from hand to mouth. A person of *ptoches* is destitute, bereft of the necessities to even sustain life. Whoever falls to this depth is utterly without resources and must depend on the largesse of others or perish. The street person who huddles on a city grate or lives in a cardboard hut is *ptoches.*

The material destitution suggested by the word *ptoches* is frightening enough. But Jesus adds an entirely new dimension of foreboding to the word when he uses it in a spiritual sense. His implication is that there is an inner destitution analogous to material *ptoches,* a spiritual poverty that strips us of internal resources and makes us helplessly dependent for our spiritual survival on something other than ourselves.

Material destitution renders us frightfully vulnerable to the whims of our external environment. A sudden cold snap, an unsympathetic cop, or a run-in with street hooligans can send us over the edge. Spiritual destitution is also a state of unspeakable frailty. It renders us as naked and exposed on the inside as a street person is on the outside. If we are *ptochos* in a material sense, we can try to cope by falling back on inner resolve and fortitude. But spiritual *ptoches* takes away even these psychological defenses. Broken in body, broken in spirit, there is nowhere safe to go.

A second, complementary way of thinking of precarity is in terms of what the theologian Johannes Metz calls the "poverty of provisionality." As historical creatures, we are constantly on the move, trailing a long past that is over and done and facing an uncertain because not-yet-happened future. We may long to hunker down and stay in place, but this kind of stasis is impossible. What we are at any present moment is always a flowing toward the future. Thus we are provisional, contingent, not yet complete. To be human is to "face the risk of a future that is yet to be," and this entails that our fundamental way of being is more along the lines of "not quite yet" than "solidly here and now."[11]

Spiritual poverty and temporal provisionality: twin characteristics of precarity. The one suggests radical vulnerability because of interior destitution, the other radical vulnerability because of a necessarily incomplete present and uncertain future. Yet Jesus claims that whoever experiences them is truly blessed, and Dorothy Day calls them graces worth praying for. How could this possibly be? Any person in his or her right mind ought to dread spiritual poverty and dig in even deeper

behind a security barrier to avoid it. Any rational person ought
to jump at the chance to avoid the anxiety caused by an
uncertain future.

Or so, at any rate, concludes the wisdom of the world. But
the subversive message that Jesus brings is twofold: poverty
and provisionality allow us to *be* more fully, and ought to be
embraced rather than feared; and God is truly found in the
midst of the poor and the provisional. The burning bush is
located in the desert of ground zero, as Methodist Bishop Joe
Pennel discovered when he visited the terrorist-bombed
Pentagon. "I met Christ," he said afterward. "We believe that
Christ is with the broken in a unique way and that Christ
dwells in suffering in a unique way. I felt the presence of Christ
there."[12]

Revelation and Salvation

Bishop Pennel's sensing of Christ's presence in the midst of
brokenness and suffering attests to the deep Christian conviction that God is found through, and not despite, precarity.
God is found in the outback, on the windswept plain and dry
salvages, not in tightly garrisoned fortresses and bulwarks.

When limit situations strip us of our usual defenses and
leave us forlornly destitute, all the obstacles that earlier
blocked our receptivity to God's presence are removed.
Similarly, when crisis circumstances force us to admit the
provisional, not-yet-complete nature of our existence, we have
nothing to fall back on but the hope that the unknown future
toward which our present moments inexorably flow is God
filled. The first creates an open space in us that makes room
for revelation. The second moves us in the direction of salvation. And both events, as Dorothy Day knew, are moments of
grace.

Revelation. The openness to God created by *ptoches* is
sometimes called "self-detachment" or "self-forgetfulness."
Adherents of safety spiritualities never really forget themselves.
There is an obvious reason for this: the whole point is to
protect the self at all costs, so it is necessarily always center
stage, under close watch and ringed round by an elaborate
arsenal of defensive shields. These shields are ultimately
incapable of protecting the self. But they *can* block out the still
small voice of God. It's difficult to hear God's whispers when
the self is stridently booming out orders.

And the self *will* noisily strut its authority, because for the
adherent of a safety spirituality, the self competes with God for
primacy of place. Security becomes an urgent need only when
the self is valued above everything else, including God. Safety
spiritualities substitute self for God as their object of ultimate
concern.

That's why Christ taught that the one sure way to enter into
communion with God is to loosen our anxious grip on strategies of self-preservation (cf. Mt 10:39). Forget the self, detach
from its panicky demands for safety zones and security barriers. Annihilate the self so that God may become all. Sink into
poverty so that there is nothing left to lose. Embrace destitution so that self-possession doesn't dull your receptivity to the
divine word. Let the old ego-protecting security barriers
collapse so that God can get through (cf. Col 3:3-4). As John
Main reminds us, "When we are renouncing self we are in that
condition of liberty and receptivity that allows us to be in
relationship with the Other."[13] And in renouncing self, we
become poor enough to receive God. As Oscar Romero once
wrote:

> The poor person is the one who has been
> converted to God and puts all his faith in him,

and the rich person is one who has not been
converted to God and puts his confidence in
idols: money, power, material things. . . . Our
work should be directed toward converting
ourselves and all people to this authentic meaning of poverty.[14]

Annihilation of self and the fall into destitution are and will
remain frightening: how could we not fear precarity? Sea
storms are always fearsome when we are caught in the middle
of them. But because self-annihilation and destitution are the
necessary conditions for genuine life, the wounds they inflict
are also great blessings. They sensitize the heart to God's
voice, thereby making us better hearers of the word. This
interior attunement makes all the difference in the world.
Without it, we visit a disaster scene and see nothing but rubble
and pointless suffering, experience nothing but panic and
anger. What if this kind of devastation should fall upon *me?*
With it, we discern God's suffering presence in the midst of
ruin and pain because the ever timid "me" is no longer the
focus of attention, blocking spiritual vision by projecting its
own anxieties and self-preoccupied fears. Such undistracted
openness doesn't lessen the horror of disasters. God forbid we
should ever trivialize the suffering of humanity, or of God. But
the new focus does allow us to see that each tragedy is a
replay of the cross, and that Christ is on each one of those
crosses.

This is the grand revelation that breaks in upon us when we
venture out of our terror-filled bunkers, brave the open places,
and in our destitution see the landscape as it really is: that God
mysteriously stands with us and shares our fear and our pain
and our forlornness. The revelation given us isn't a magical
word of comfort or the grand unveiling of a cosmic plan that

promises us that what looks like suffering really isn't. Such easy assurances aren't what Christianity's all about. Instead, we are given something much greater: the awareness that God shares our pain and hence can be found in the midst of it.

This is incomprehensible on a rational level—foolishness to some, scandalous to others, says Saint Paul. What kind of God *suffers?* But the answer to that one is easy: a God who *loves.* As Karl Rahner points out, the essence of the divine "permanent mystery" given in revelation is this: God is incomprehensible and inexhaustible love, love so intense that God sacrificially self-abandons in reaching out to us.[15] Love, of course, is always risky, because love demands sacrifice of self for the sake of the beloved. We are God's beloved, and hence God's risk. Out of sheer love, God abandons Godself in the incarnational emptying. God relinquishes divine prerogative in order to be Immanuel, God with us. God becomes vulnerable, experiences pain and ultimately a scoundrel's death on the cross. And this is the very God forever present in crises, in limit situations, on the margins, in the rubble. God chooses, out of sheer love, to renounce security—which has no patience with taking risks of any kind—and to share our precarity.

When brought to our knees by limit situations such as 9/11, we are offered a great opportunity to experience God by meeting God in the midst of the spiritual poverty God and we share, the poverty of the cross, the utter destitution that led the dying Jesus to cry out in despairing abandonment. Like beckons to like, affinity calls to affinity. The more Godlike we become—that is, the more destitute of the "me" and its distracting clamor for security—the better we are able to experience God. Once we step out of the safety zone into the margins, once we hazard risky love, the God of the margins self-reveals.

Then we discover what we could never have guessed
ensconced in safety spiritualities: we only genuinely receive
and return God's love when we accept God for who God is.
This requires giving up our frightened insistence on clinging to
an idea of God as the Cosmic Fixer. Safety spiritualities are no
longer possible once we step out into the open. God's job is
not to coddle us but to liberate us from our timid need for
coddling. Thus Jesus admonished Mary not to cling to him,
and later he warned the disciples that they mustn't use him as
a crutch. "It is expedient for you that I go away, for if I go not
away the Holy Spirit cannot come unto you" (Acts 1:8).

To repeat: love is a risky business. God takes a colossal risk
in loving timid, unpredictable creatures like us. We, in turn,
take a risk in receiving and returning that love, in placing
ourselves in the hands of a God who cannot and does not
promise to keep us from harm's way. What God *does* promise
is to love us steadfastly, to share our vulnerability, and to hurt
alongside us in the rubble.

Christianity's extraordinary spiritual insight that to love God
means embracing the insecurity of living on the divine margin
is, in Alan Watts's opinion, nothing less than "revolutionary."
It forces us to grapple with

> The incredible truth that what religion calls the
> vision of God is found in giving up any belief in
> [an abstract] idea of God. By the same law of
> reversed effort, we discover the "infinite" and the
> "absolute," not by straining to escape from the
> finite and relative world, but by the most com-
> plete acceptance of its limitations.[16]

God reveals to us in the here and now of a finite, relative, and
hence messy and dangerous world. This is the God who loves
us, and this is the God we are called to love, not some abstract

idea of God the Protector that may be more comforting but, as Freud would say, is wishful thinking.

Salvation. Precarity means becoming spiritually poor enough to accept the revelation that God is the self-giving Love found on the other side of safety zones and security barriers. We find God in the destitution of *ptoches,* and in finding God we discover that God, too, is *ptoches.* As Saint Paul knew, God's power is manifested in and through what the world misguidedly dismisses as weakness (cf. 2 Cor 12:8).

Revelation is always accompanied by the offer of salvation. An embrace of spiritual *poverty* opens us to God's presence in the here and now. An embrace of *provisionality* moves us toward a trusting reliance on God's future will. Poverty prepares us for the revelation of risky love, provisionality for the hope of salvation.

Recall what provisionality means: that humans are not-yet-complete creatures, always flowing into an uncertain and hence anxiety-provoking future. Because of our deep dread of insecurity, we typically resist this provisionality by pretending that our destiny is in our control. In the material realm we fancy that we can control the future by manipulating the present: a college degree now guarantees a well-paying job later; a strong military buildup now forestalls future terrorist attacks. We make similar presumptions in the spiritual realm: lots of praying now means holiness later on; good deeds in the present bring a future heaven.

But our efforts to determine the future and thus complete ourselves under our own steam are futile because they rest on the false assumption that the future is somehow in our control. Strategies for determining the course of the future in effect aim at making the future merely an extension of the present—a new wing added to our spiritual fortress, if you will. But as we have seen, even the tangible present isn't in our control. How much less, then, the intangible future.

What we must confess is what we already know in our heart of hearts: the future can't be crammed into the confines of our safety spiritualities. We should acknowledge that we are irremediably provisional (at least in this life), always on the move, always traveling from one point to another, and that this provisionality necessarily makes the future unpredictable and hazardous. But at the same time, we should also confess what even the most timid of us feel in our deepest core: the future is also mysteriously appealing, beckoning us in our very provisionality, drawing us toward it even as we resist it. Johannes Metz describes the strange dynamic this way:

> I do not belong to myself; I am a stranger to myself, a no-man's land between the past prom- ise and the still to come fulfillment. I have nothing to make me strong or rich. Everything within me strains forward, is set on edge in prophetic anticipation . . . of an intangible future, and I am to find therein my true self, the prom- ised land of my Father.[17]

If Metz is correct, the uncertain future beckons to us, even as it frightens us, because we sense that it can complete our merely provisional natures if we give ourselves over to it. And what else could possibly do this but God—the God who awaits us just over the temporal horizon, just on the other side of our present-momented safety zones? Embracing our provisionality means putting ourselves in the hands of something that awaits us in the future which is greater than anything we can imag- ine. It means to stop playing it safe by trying to determine the future and instead to throw ourselves into the uncertainty—

with "prophetic anticipation," as Metz says—trusting that the God of the margins who loves us unconditionally will catch us. The anxiety remains. But when we cease resisting our inherent provisionality, it is accompanied with hope and longing. As Richard Rohr wisely says, this hope ultimately "calls us to destroy our idols, our defense mechanisms, and it leads us to trust in God alone. His love gives us the security to be insecure, to let go of the present and head toward the future."[18]

In more traditional terms, embracing our provisionality is a necessary step for allowing ourselves to be guided by God's will rather than insisting on our own (which, when we think about it, is itself a kind of poverty). There will come a time, Jesus told Peter (and, by implication, the rest of us), when you'll be led in directions you haven't chosen, bound by a will greater than your own, thrust into a future you wouldn't necessarily have selected of your own accord (cf. Jn 21:18-19).

These are fearsome words to those of us so fearful of losing control that we struggle to twist the not-yet future into just an extension of the present. But once we recognize that the future is the place of our salvation, that the future is the fulfillment of our not-yet-complete nature, we get rid, as Stanley Hauerwas writes, "of the notion that the world exists indefinitely, that we have a stake in the preservation of the world-as-is."[19] The world-as-is is only a prelude to the world-as-it-will-be, a world opened to us by our provisional relation to a future that flows from and back toward saving Love.

Treading Water, Floating on God

It is remarkable that we fear the very thing that can save us, but so it is. We are graced with precarity, and by this gift are gloriously bound to God in two ways. First, our innate

provisionality and potential spiritual poverty signal our radical
dependence on the divine Other. Second, our precarity links
us to God because God shares the same quality by virtue of
God's unconditional and risky love for creation. We should
revere the wound of precarity, for it is a blessed one. In it,
God reveals and we are saved—but only if we have opened the
eye of the heart to discern what is going on.

Martin Luther once wrote that security is the ultimate idol.
We so long for security that we will bow before it, offer up to it
our firstborn, and freeze our future into an ever-present now
for its sake. In worshiping this golden calf we squander our
energy by frantically throwing up security barriers when what
we ought to be doing is venturing out into the open, just as
God did when God risked dwelling among us. We are not
made for safety spiritualities, for hunkering down or dodging
risk. We are lovingly made for love, and to love is to accept
insecurity and risk and vulnerability for the sake of Love.
There is no painlessness in a love-ruled world, and that's
necessarily frightening. But it is also a reasonable price to pay.
Even God has to ante up for the sake of love.

In the Introduction I noted that limit situations, those crises
that serve as opportunities for self- and God-discovery, are
frequently symbolized in scripture as storms at sea. The
Anglican theologian John Macquarrie correctly reminds us that
even when we are not being tossed about by wind and waves,
we still tread water. Our lives may seem placid and safe as a
becalmed sea, but we are always at risk. Precarity is the
human condition:

> [When] people ask me, "Did Jesus really walk on
> the sea?" I reply, "I've been walking myself on
> the water for quite a few decades. I've often been
> sinking, but like Peter I've found that faith keeps

one afloat." "Walking on water" is a perfect
description of the human condition. . . .

But, Macquarrie goes on to say, precarity is also the *divine*
condition:

> The story of Christ walking on the water is not a
> story of his supernatural power but rather an
> illustration of how in his humanity he shared all
> the insecurity and vulnerability of our earthly
> life.[20]

Dorothy Day made the same point about Christ's vulnerability, and ours, in as striking a passage as she ever wrote:

> We are told to put on Christ and we think of Him
> in His private life, His life of work, His public life,
> His teaching and His suffering life. But we do not
> think enough of His life as a little child, as a
> baby. His helplessness. His powerlessness. We
> have to be content to be in that state too. Not to
> be able to do anything, to accomplish anything.[21]

In accepting who we are, in crawling out of our safety spiritualities to acknowledge our own essential precarity, we tread the waters of existence—which in turn lie atop the deep, bottomless waters of God—with fear and trembling, joy and hope. Sea storms come and go. But the divine ocean endures.

⊰ 2 ⊱

Seeing
and Thanking

For a Christian the sin is to
lose the perspective of God.
—OSCAR ROMERO

Angle of Vision

Philosopher Martin Heidegger once argued that thinking,
rightly understood, is also an act of thanking. The reason for
this is that proper thinking—not, as we'll see a bit later in this
chapter, what conventionally passes for thinking—is the act of
receiving something welcome, and this always implies gratitude on the part of the receiver.[1]

Thinking in Heidegger's sense is somewhat analogous to
vision, or the act of seeing. The eye is our window to the
world, and seeing reveals to us what the world is all about. If
the window is clean, what we see in the world is God, and this
in turn makes us thankful. But if the window is smeared for
one reason or another, we squint through a glass darkly. Either
our own smudged reflection stares back at us, or we can catch
only vague glimpses of those images on the other side. But
because they are befouled by the dirtiness of the window, they
are causes for anxiety if not outright alarm rather than gratitude.

Christianity is all about looking at the world in a new way. One of Jesus' favorite words is "behold," and in inviting us to "behold," he offers a therapy by which we learn how to see. His good news is that the windows through which we view reality can be cleaned, and that a genuine relationship with what *is,* rather than with what we merely *imagine* to be, can be attained. When it is, our new way of seeing allows us to rethink the world. In rethinking it, we rediscover just how much there is to be grateful for. "Let us come into his presence with thanksgiving" (Ps 95:2).

The new way of seeing/thinking/thanking offered by the Christian vision is only possible once we find the courage to step out from behind our security barriers and gaze at the world unburdened by the usual armor we wear. As we saw in the last chapter, that armor doesn't really protect us anyway. Instead, it only dulls our senses and blocks our vision. We can't feel cool water or warm spring air for the sheets of metal covering our bodies. The visor on our clunky helmet narrows our perspective, making us, as Dorothy Day once noted, the "blindest of the blind."

But when we strip down—when we embrace the way of precarity and open ourselves to the possibility of revelation and salvation—the world looks quite different. Instead of viewing it from the perspective of a visored adversary, we view it from the perspective of a grateful friend. We see it a bit as the God who loved it into being and called it good sees it. And that, as Archbishop Romero said, is precisely the angle of vision Christians ought to desire.

Carpe Diem?

Everybody knows, and many claim as their own, the old Latin tag *carpe diem,* "seize the day." For most of us, the expression is a reminder to suck as much experience out of each passing moment as we possibly can. We only go around once, we say, so we should get what we can out of life.

Despite its undertone of anxiety—so much to do, so little time to do it—this popular interpretation of *carpe diem* is innocent enough. But it is not quite what the Roman poet Horace had in mind when he first penned the phrase. He intended a darker, more somber meaning, one that sheds a good deal of light on the way safety spiritualities encourage us to see the world.

Horace's first "Ode," in which the phrase appears, is (in part) a melancholy reflection on the frailty and vanity of human existence—a Latin Ecclesiastes, if you will. In recommending *carpe diem,* Horace says this:

> fill not
> Your bosom with large hopes; for while I sing,
> The envious close of time is narrowing;—
> So seize the day, or ever it be past,
> And let the morrow come for what it will.[2]

The message of these lines is as obvious as it is bleak: time itself is an adversary against which we must maintain continuous vigilance. Wise persons, recognizing fully well how short life is, will seize the fleeing moment and bid it stay longer. They will try to protect themselves by freezing, or at least delaying, time.

The basic attitude behind Horace's *carpe diem* is that humans are engaged in a war against the great enemy time—a war, by the way, that we must inevitably lose. Time races forward with roller-coaster speed, dragging us unwillingly along until it abruptly dumps us out at some point along the way. The best we can do is struggle against our merciless foe by trying to stall its progress. But we can never secure our perimeters permanently, and this sickening realization only makes us more anxious to "seize the day." This anxiety ultimately defines our existence: each of us is trapped in the struggle to block the passage of time, to grab for ourselves a safely captured respite in which to catch our breath. It also defines the world in which we live as the bleak battlefield on which our campaign against time must be fought.

Horace's horror at the swiftness of time shouldn't be confused with the anxiety that arises from the provisionality to which Johannes Metz drew our attention in the previous chapter. As we saw, provisionality alarms us because it hurls us into an uncertain future. But Horace isn't worried about what the future holds so much as the ephemerality of the present moment, the fact that time ceaselessly slips through our fingers. The point here is the instability of the now, not the unknowability of the future.

Those of us who try to put a festive spin on *carpe diem* are well reminded of Horace's original intent. For what passes today as a carefree grab-all-the-gusto-you-can attitude is often a sadly frenetic effort to deny the darker side of existence. Life isn't a beer commercial, no matter how much we try to pretend otherwise. The vast energy we put into distracting ourselves through entertainment attests to the fact that we are incredibly anxious about the ephemerality of time and much prefer to have our attention deflected.[3] There is frequently a grim, clenched-jaw quality to our determination to find amusement and forget our worries. So even the contemporary don't-worry-be-happy reading of *carpe diem* has a certain despair embedded in it.

Our need to halt time and hence protect ourselves from its roller-coaster ride clearly exhibits itself in our everyday lives on

a regular basis. We take countless snapshots while on holiday
or at festive events, fancying that we can somehow seize and
save the moment. At particularly pleasurable moments we
wistfully murmur, "I wish this could last forever!" as if somehow the quality of the moment is compromised by its transitory nature. We spend billions of dollars each year in attempts
to make ourselves look younger than we actually are and
thereby trick ourselves into thinking we have vanquished time.
And we constantly consult our watches and clocks to see
where their hands point. We're like Jonathan Swift's Gulliver,
who paid homage to his timepiece so frequently that the
uncomprehending Lilliputians thought the strange object he
kept pulling out of his pocket must surely be his god.

Speaking of gods, our fear of temporality also expresses
itself spiritually. In our religious moods, just as in our secular
ones, we declare temporality the great enemy, insisting that it
is the source of all the worldly cares and worries that distract
us from fixing our gaze on God. We convince ourselves that
God is outside the temporal flow and that we, accordingly,
should refocus our attention on atemporal things—things "of
the spirit." Defeat the temporal by shooting for the eternal.
Forsake the world of flux and flow for an empyrean realm of
changeless perfection. Only there, sunk deeply within the
protective enclave of timelessness, can we find the spiritual
security we crave.

This kind of spirituality is obviously otherworldly in the
extreme. It exhorts us to keep our distance from the things of
this world, ruled as they are by the great enemy time. Fixing
our eyes on the prize of heaven not only enables us to roll
more easily with time's punches, but it also reassures us that
horrendous events—limit situations such as 9/11—somehow
aren't real in the same way that God's never-changing eternal

order is real. Catastrophes like terrorist attacks or cancer or bankruptcy come and go, but eternity remains. Temporal assaults may strike us on the surface, but they can't break through to where it really counts: that interior safety zone deep within—call it the *soul*—where we are securely impregnable.

It is obvious that an otherworldly spirituality that seeks to deny the reality of time necessarily disparages the value of particular objects and events and people, since all these exist in time and derive their identity in part from their temporal environment. Time-denying spiritualities are too pristine for the rough edge of mundane affairs. They prefer to bypass the messiness of the here and now and cut straight to the immaculate ice palace of timelessness.

In both spiritual and nonspiritual spheres, then, we see the same tendency: the urge to immobilize time so that we can feel more securely rooted. There is no question here of looking at the world around us, thinking, and thanking. On the contrary, to think about the world is to be threatened. Our sense of safety depends on our ability to control the external environment, and time is that environment's most obviously dangerous loose cannon. By focusing away from passing moments to an ever-nowed present, we dam the river of time that erodes our banks—or so, at any rate, we fancy. This need to destroy time—which, of course, is a defense mechanism birthed by our deep-seated fear of insecurity—is Medusa-like. It seeks to solidify something that is dynamic and fluid and living—the temporal world, the realm of human experience, and, first and foremost, God—into static, immobile, and dead stone. Stone is cold to the touch and makes for a most uncomfortable pillow. But it does give the illusion of impregnability.[4]

Catch Them if You Can

American Quaker mystic and activist Rufus Jones was well aware of the temptation to play it safe by barricading oneself against the slippage of time. But he insisted that this attitude was particularly inconsistent with Christianity's way of seeing the world.

In one of his best books, *New Eyes for Invisibles,* Jones focuses on a text from Saint Paul that, on first reading, appears to fall into the time-denial characteristic of safety spiritualities. "We look not at what can be seen," writes Paul, speaking to his fellow Christians, "but at what cannot be seen; for what can be seen is temporary, but what cannot be seen is eternal" (2 Cor 4:18).

What Paul is describing here (and prescribing, too) is a new kind of vision, one that allows us to pick up on aspects of reality we normally miss. We tend to look no further than our noses, consciously seeing only those things we have been conditioned to focus on. What we need to do is cultivate a new kind of vision that lets us see "invisibles" as well.

According to Jones, this new vision must be "bifocaled" so that we see both "visibles" and "invisibles" with equally clear vision. It's no good focusing on one at the expense of the other. Both are necessary, if we would see reality as it truly is. Jones grants that Paul's wording might give the impression that he wants to bypass the visibles altogether. But this, Jones explains, should be read as an instance of "oriental over-emphasis":

> Paul is so impressed with the importance of
> seeing invisible realities that he tells us not to
> look at the things that are seen. But we should

probably never find the invisibles if we wholly
neglected the visible world. We are more apt to
find the invisible Reals by looking *through* the
visibles, as the medium. We should never have
discovered the laws of the universe if we had
neglected to observe the objects through which
the laws are revealed. What St. Paul would say if
he were here now would be something like this:
"You belong to two worlds; do not miss the
invisible one while you are busy with the visible
one. Cultivate your vision, learn to see the
realities which your eyes miss. Look through the
world that is seen and discover the realities which
it suggests and implies."[5]

Jones reminds us here that the Christian way of looking at
the world is incarnational through and through. Earlier Greek
metaphysics taught that reality is a two-tiered system with time
and change on the lower level, eternity and changelessness on
the upper, and no elevator in between. But Christianity isn't
similarly dualistic. It affirms—it celebrates—that in pitching a
tent in our midst, God once and for all infused the Eternal into
each passing moment, each seemingly ordinary event in the
world. The upper story collapsed in on the lower one, so that
to see God now, one need only look at the temporal world.
No elevator is needed, because the Incarnation has eliminated
clear-cut distinctions between the timeless sacred and the
timed profane.

It only makes sense, as Jones says, that if we really know
how to see visibles, invisibles are necessarily revealed within
them and through them. Temporal visibles are the media by
which God is present to us. In serving as the frames of God's
self-revelation, they take on a value and beauty that, once

noticed, cannot but fill us with wonder and gratitude. When
this happens, the visibles—everything that flows in the unstop-
pable river of time, everything that comes, lingers for but an
instant, and then departs—are no longer threatening. They
are, instead, all the more dear to us because of the glimpses of
invisibles they grant before drifting away on time's current.
Time, according to this way of seeing the world, isn't the great
enemy. Rather, it is the medium through which eternity
beckons to us. It is the bringer of glad tidings. This, of course,
is similar to Alan Watts's insight, mentioned in the previous
chapter, that the "infinite" must be found in the "finite and
relative world."

Behind Jones's insistence that we can apprehend and
appreciate the eternal only through the temporal is a doctrine
theologians sometimes call the scandal of particularity, the
claim that the universal is revealed only in and through the
particular. This is a scandal on two counts. First, it offends
reason. How can that which by definition is limited and time-
bound possibly provide a conduit for the infinite and eternal?
Second, it affronts our timid need for safe margins and clearly
defined borders. People are tempted by safety spiritualities
because they crave pristine order with everything in its desig-
nated place: heaven "up there," untouchable by the chaos
"down here." But in an incarnate universe, in a cosmos where
God is an actual inhabitant rather than an absentee landlord,
these prissy kinds of demarcations aren't to be found.

Like it or not, that is simply the way things are. We are
particular creatures who have particular experiences in a
particularized world. As Annie Dillard once noted, the "scandal
of particularity is the only world that I, in particular, know. . . .
We're all up to our necks in this particular scandal. . . . I never
saw a tree that was no tree in particular."[6] To hold out for an
experience of timeless universals unfiltered through timed

particulars is not only to indulge in a futile commanding of the tide to cease. It is also to devalue the rich world of finite experiences in which we live. And what are we holding out for anyway? A realm that is not even imaginable. "I never met a man," Dillard continues, "not [even] the greatest theologian, who filled infinity, or even whose hand, say, was undifferentiated, fingerless, like a griddle cake, and not lobed and split just so with the incursions of time."[7]

Dillard's point is worth considering. Particularity shouldn't frighten us as much as it does. It is, after all, what we know and who we are. What *should* scare us is precisely what we, in our timidity, *think* we want: a frozen reality where the perspective and differentiation granted by time is eliminated. *Carpe diem.* But how could one possibly orient oneself in such a bizarre world? How could one make one's way? How could one breathe in a petrified forest of universals?

Jones and Dillard agree that the God for whom we yearn can't be found by stepping outside of the temporal flow but only by learning to see God's presence in its midst. Both of them admit that such encounters will necessarily be transitory. As we saw in the last chapter, God is found on the fragile, crumbly margins. But Jones and Dillard also attest from personal experience that these encounters, brief as they may be, are still enough to smash through our timid reserve. "Suddenly I felt the walls between the visible and the invisible grow thin and the Eternal seemed to break through into the world where I was," says Jones while admiring the beauty of the Swiss Alps.[8] Annie Dillard, gazing at a sunset in the mountains of Virginia, has a similar reaction. "I am more alive than all the world," she remarks in wonderment.[9]

When God self-reveals in the particular moment, we find ourselves standing before the burning bush in all our nakedness, utterly vulnerable, all guards down, defense strategies forgotten—and, most astonishingly, we couldn't care less. During moments like these we fully appreciate just how far fear can exile us from the Promised Land. We know that such moments can't be frozen, and that if they could, they would no longer be worth much of anything. "Catch them if you can," Dillard teasingly says, knowing all along that we can't, and shouldn't try.

Holiness in the Present Moment

We should rethink *carpe diem* in light of Dillard's "catch them if you can." A more appropriate reading of it than "seize the day" would be "celebrate the moment without trying to freeze it." Realize that human experiences, transitory as they necessarily are, nonetheless are laden with the eternity for which we thirst. Know, furthermore, that it is only in the passing moment—the particular—that the eternal reveals itself to us, and that if we try to hang onto the moment because our deep woundedness causes us to fear time's slippage, we lose both it and the eternal that shimmers through it.

Gregory of Nyssa, meditating on the line "Give us this day our daily bread" in the *Pater Noster,* realizes that it is much more than just a petition for food. At a deeper level, it is also the hope that we might be satisfied with what the moment brings without needing to reach out and grab hold of time. The ancient Hebrews were fed with manna, a victual so fragile that it never lasted more than a day. Hoarding it for the purpose of controlling the food supply was useless. It simply vanished, teaching Moses and his people to take the present seriously.[10]

In our own day Anthony de Mello appeals to the following story to underscore the spiritual importance of appreciating the present without trying to control it:

> Buddha was once asked, "What makes a person
> holy?" He replied, "Every hour is divided into a
> certain number of seconds and every second into
> a certain number of fractions. Anyone who is
> able to be totally present in each fraction of a
> second is holy."[11]

Total presence in the now, says de Mello, is holiness. But this
kind of total presence is only possible if we can control our
anxious need to grab time (remember Jacob the "grabber"?)
and bend it to our will.

Saying this is one thing. Knowing how to go about it is
another. So it is perfectly appropriate to ask just how one
succeeds in making oneself totally present to the now. And to
answer that, it is helpful, by way of analogy, to reflect on what
it means to be present to another person.

When I meet another person, there are four fundamental
ways in which I can respond. To begin with, I can be com-
pletely indifferent, sizing the person up as nothing more than
a kind of animated object unworthy of my attention. Second, I
can see the person as an animated tool that I can bend to my
own will. Indifference gives way here to interest, but the
interest is purely instrumental. Third, I can respond to the
other as a threatening adversary who needs to be vanquished
quickly. Finally, I can see the person as a human being in
whom God dwells.

In the first three responses, I refuse to make myself present
to the other. In reducing the person to nothing more than an
object, by either ignoring or trying to be controlling and
manipulative, I shut myself off from the possibility of meaningful contact. I'm no more present than I would be to a vacuum
cleaner or a pesky gnat. Making myself present to and for

another human requires an appreciative openness, a receptivity, an attentiveness, and an empathic availability that we simply don't extend to mere things. Being present to another not only permits that person to reveal himself or herself to me. It also gives me the opportunity to be enriched by the revelation. (We will explore this point more deeply in the next chapter.)

When our deep woundedness compels us to so crave safety and security that we manically "seize the day," we respond to the ephemeral present as either an enemy or, at best, as an object to be nailed down, held in place, and made to serve us. In our panic to stop the present from slipping away, we close ourselves off from what it might have to reveal. We treat it as merely a temporal phenomenon—a timed "thing"—and in our rush either to flee or control refuse to cultivate a receptivity to it. As a consequence, we are never even partially present to the now and, following de Mello, our lives are not holy.

Both Ralph Waldo Emerson and Martin Heidegger offer helpful insights about our fear-inspired tendency to seize time. Emerson claims that the "evanescence and lubricity" of timed existence so upsets us that we *clutch* with all our might to keep it from "slip[ping] through our fingers." The word "clutch" is particularly appropriate in this context, because it connotes panic and desperation; a drowning person "clutches" at anything. The frenzy with which we clutch at evanescent and lubricious time is, concludes Emerson, "the most unhandsome part of our condition."[12]

Heidegger likewise sees "clutching" *(greifen)* as the way of responding most characteristic of frightened insecurity. Clutching in some contexts may be perfectly appropriate. The human hand, after all, is anatomically much more suited for clutching than any other "grasping organ" such as paw, claw,

or fang, and we ought to take advantage of its superiority
when occasion calls. But the problem is that we use the hand's
ability to clutch as a model for *all* our responses to existence.
We begin to confuse the act of thinking with the act of clutching (thinking becomes, says Heidegger, a *handi*craft) and
presume that our response to the world in general and to time
in particular ought to be one of grabbing and controlling. Like
Emerson, Heidegger considers this an unhandsome condition.
His own name for it is "challenging-forth," a perpetually
adversarial attitude that sees and treats the world as a threatening foe that must be defeated.[13]

Both Emerson and Heidegger, then, argue that the at-
tempt to seize the day is a kind of sublimized violence in
which we don't so much make ourselves present to the now
as closed-off foes of it. That this is a fear-based strategy
rather than a natural one is evidenced by the fact that we are
also strangely attracted to the present moment. As Heidegger
puts it, the now draws us into itself as sea creatures are
drawn into the wake of a ship. We may struggle against the
attraction, but in fact we long to give way to it.[14] The reason
for the attraction to the present moment is not unlike the
attraction to the future we examined in Chapter 1. Despite
our panicked need to freeze the one and forestall the other,
our deeper intuitions whisper that God is to be found in the
fleeing now, just as in the unknown future. And the only
possible ground of those kinds of intuitions is our experience
of the scandal of particularity: somehow the eternal universal
for which we ache is found precisely in the transient particular we so fear.

Both Emerson and Heidegger argue that what we must do
is cultivate presence or receptivity to the temporal now in
order to glimpse the eternal—the *God*—it conveys. In trying

to describe what this state of being is like, Emerson invokes his famous image of the "transparent eyeball":

> Crossing a bare common, in snow puddles, at
> twilight, under a clouded sky, without having in
> my thoughts any occurrence of special good
> fortune, I have enjoyed a perfect exhilaration. I
> am glad to the brink of fear. . . . Standing on the
> bare ground—my head bathed by the blithe air,
> and uplifted into infinite space— all mean
> egotism vanishes. I become a transparent eye-
> ball; I am nothing; I see all; the currents of the
> universal Being circulate through me; I am part
> or parcel of God.[15]

Two features of Emerson's description are worth pointing out. In the first place, and perhaps most striking, is the suggestion that becoming fully present to the now is a cause of "exhilaration" rather than panic. If fear can be attributed to the experience at all, it is only when speaking about the almost unbearable sense of joy it brings. Tossing our wounded caution to the wind and allowing ourselves to sink into the present moment without trying to control it frees us to discover something quite different from what we in our timidity antici-pated.

Second, Emerson seems to be suggesting that a necessary condition for becoming present to the now is that we shuck off, as a snake casts off its skin, that constellation of inhibitions, ambitions, fears, and fantasies that is our ego. His experience of entering into the now doesn't seem to be an act intended and performed by his "me." Rather, it is an event— an act of grace, if you will—that happens to him unexpectedly

as he crosses a common on a gray winter's day. Emerson's
normal defenses are down, the security barriers are lowered,
and his receptivity proportionately increased. As we saw in
Chapter 1, this "me-less" state, in which we let go (or better,
are granted the boon of letting go) of the ego and all its petty
concerns, is what Jesus called spiritual poverty. It is a dwelling
on the margins of "me-ness," a place of great precarity and,
accordingly, a place of great revelation.

This egolessness increases our receptivity because, to use
an image favored by Zen Buddhists, it helps us to become
"empty mirrors"—immaculately transparent panes through
which the sunlight passes and, in passing, fills. This transparency refocuses our vision, allowing us to discern something in
the passing moment of such wondrous substance that it can
only be called, as Emerson unhesitatingly calls it, God. And
this discernment is quite impossible if, instead of opening
oneself to the now, one desperately tries to freeze it. The
point here is to let go, to cease striving, to allow the moment
to approach, wash over one's senses, and then recede into the
distance. As anyone who has ever stargazed knows, peripheral
vision often reveals more than staring straight at the intended
object.

Annie Dillard, who earlier introduced us to the phrase
"scandal of particularity," has experienced this sort of transparency, this presence to the now, and wonderfully described
it in her *Pilgrim at Tinker Creek*. She tells us that she had
pulled into a gas station in "Nowhere, Virginia" and was
sipping a cup of coffee, absentmindedly petting a puppy, and
staring at the sun going down behind the Blue Ridge Mountains while the station attendant checked her oil. Her mind
was blank from the weariness of a day of driving. She wasn't
consciously thinking about anything, much less aware of
herself. And then it happened. Her senses, inner as well as

outer, opened themselves to the present moment, and in so doing discovered a world of beauty and wonder:

> Shadows lope along the mountain's rumpled flanks; they elongate like root tips, like lobes of spilling water, faster and faster. A warm purple pigment pools in each ruck and tuck of the rock; it deepens and spreads, boring crevasses, canyons. As the purple vaults and slides, it tricks out the unleafed forest and rumpled rock in gilt, in shape-shifting patches of glow. These gold lights veer and retract, shatter and glide in a series of dazzling splashes, shrinking, leaking, exploding. The ridge's bosses and hummocks sprout bulging from its side; the whole mountain looms miles closer; the light warms and reddens; the bare forest folds and pleats itself like living protoplasm before my eyes.[16]

It is at this point that Dillard exultantly pronounced herself "more alive than all the world." The entire creation suddenly unveiled to her as a vital, living, and unspeakably beautiful whole, and all because she ceased pursuing the ever elusive present and simply allowed it to be. The majesty of the moment—living protoplasm, living God—overwhelmed her. "This is it," she remembers thinking, "right now, the present, this empty gas station, here, this western wind, this tang of coffee on the tongue, and I am patting the puppy, I am watching the mountain." And then, with this return of self-awareness, the moment passed on. "The second I verbalize this awareness in my brain, I cease to see the mountain or feel the puppy. I am opaque, so much black asphalt."[17] Transparency gave way to opaqueness, presence-to-the-moment destroyed by the ego's knee-jerk (and jerky) lust to be in control. But the memory of connection remained, guaranteeing that the experience was real and valuable:

> I sip my coffee. I look at the mountain, which is still doing its tricks, as you look at a still-beautiful face belonging to a person who was once your lover in another country years ago: with fond nostalgia, and recognition. . . . Thanks. For the memories.[18]

Such moments of undivided consciousness, of absorbing the present moment because one has achieved the receptivity of an empty mirror or a transparent eyeball, are, Dillard concludes, "our few live seasons. Let us live them as purely as we can, in the present."[19] For these seasons are holy, and make us holy.

Grateful Seeing

In our fear of insecurity, we "seize the day" by defining time as an adversary and challenging it forth to do battle. Moreover, everything temporal is seen as time's ally, and the whole world becomes one huge battlefield. When we "see" and think about creation in these terms, there is no place for wonder and gratitude in our response to the world. Our ancient wound inhibits us from looking beyond our own frantic ego-needs. But as Irenaeus reminded us centuries ago, "Nothing is a vacuum in the face of God. Everything is a sign of God."[20] God's presence shines forth from every particular. Instead of seizing the day, then, we need to celebrate it, recognizing that the God for whom we cry out is found in the now, or nowhere.

The present moment is sacramental. It is the conduit through which the eternal breaks into our lives, and its presence transfigures all of creation into something sacred. When we open ourselves to that presence, stepping outside our underground bunkers long enough to see and think it, we are given a great gift, and the only proper response to this boon is thankfulness. Heidegger once wrote that the "most thought-provoking [thing] in our thought-provoking time is that we are still not thinking."[21] On the surface, such a claim seems absurd. *Of course* we think! How else could I write or you read this book? But Heidegger isn't saying that we don't engage in calculative reasoning. Indeed, we do so all too frequently; it is the typical cognitive mode of people who dread insecurity, because it specializes in utilitarian problem-solving. Rather, Heidegger's meaning is that we fail to tap into the deeper meditative kind of thought that intuits the holiness of the present moment, receives the gift of God, and responds with wonder-filled gratitude. All *proper* thinking, Heidegger insists, is really thanking. *Denken* is *danken*. So if we "think" about ourselves and the world in ways that don't roll over into "thanking," we haven't yet begun to think properly.

This thankful thinking is a way of seeing the world as God sees the world. It is the angle of vision, as good Oscar Romero reminded us, that Christians ought to have. Our ancestors Adam and Eve looked upon creation in this receptive manner, but the vision of their descendents grew myopic until the grace of Christ enabled humans to rediscover the universal in the particular. In opening our eyes, Christ showed us that we must embrace rather than fear the temporal world's refusal to stay in one place very long, and that doing so means forsaking our neurotic addiction to security for the sake of liberating precarity. In a world that is thoroughly incarnational, there is no justification for seeing impermanence as an

enemy or particularity as a scandal. Let whoever has eyes to
see, see.

But seeing, of course, is only possible if we are awake, and
those of us who latch onto *carpe diem* as our mantra have
allowed our fear of precarity to send us into a troubled sleep
we foolishly hope will protect us from the anxiety of existence.
Of course it doesn't. But what it *does* manage to do is benumb
our senses so that we find it difficult to discern the eternal in
the particular, the divine Now in the temporal now. That's why
we usually need a grace-inspired wake-up call: Emerson's
winter common, Dillard's summer sunset. We are simply too
groggy to awaken on our own.

We ought to remember that such experiences not only help
us become more alert to God's presence in the midst of the
very precarity we so desperately try to deny. They also re-
create us in the process of awakening us. The word *waken*
has an interesting and illuminating origin. It comes from the
Old English *waecnian,* one of whose meanings, in addition to
the more conventional "to rouse out of sleep," is "to come
into being." When we grow attuned to the fact that God's
presence shimmers in the ephemeral present, and that neither
time nor the temporal world is an enemy, we become something quite different from timid bunker creatures crippled by
our ancient wound. We transfigure into creatures able to see
and think and gratefully celebrate the wide open places of
God's creation.

And the awakening, as Philip Hallie reminds us, is never
privately "ecstatic," a solitary and passive experience. Seeing
the world differently entails acting differently in it. So the
awakening that comes with an embrace of the scandal of
particularity is "not unlike the musical or poetic inspiration that
makes some people productive geniuses. Such inspiration is

not like a mystical trance; it raises people above their ordinary levels of energy, so that, celebrating, they rush out to meet and to change the world around them."[22]

Rushing out to meet and change the world instead of hunkering behind our security barriers is the topic of the final two chapters.

⊰ 3 ⊱

Beloved Community

Community [is] the harbinger
of God's Kingdom.
—EBERHARD ARNOLD, *WHY WE LIVE IN COMMUNITY*

Innocence Lost

Since terrorism came to our shores on 9/11, many of us have felt a deep need to present a united front against the threat we fear is here to stay. A lonely sense of fragility gnaws at us, and we scurry to join hands with others so that we and they might feel a bit less forlorn and hopeless. A word we frequently invoke to describe this longing for togetherness is *community.*

But, sadly, the ancient wound that maddens us with fear and drives us to entomb ourselves in suffocatingly airtight security bunkers is the single greatest obstacle to the birth of the community for which we yearn. This is tragic, because community is the only place where authentic personhood and fulfilling relationships can flourish—which is just to say that community is the only place where love, a necessary condition for personhood and relationship, abides. To be without community is to be forlornly stunted as a human being. Brazilian theologian Leonardo Boff goes so far as to say that a community-less human has lost his or her likeness to the

Trinitarian God, within whom the three Persons love one
another eternally.[1]

Love, as we have already noted, is risky business. It entices
lovers across safe boundaries into the realm of precarity,
nudging them to open up in trust and good will to others.
Community, therefore, is the place where, at one and the
same time, love and precarity dwell. Community isn't a high-
walled fortress that protects us from danger. On the contrary,
it is a place where we are probably more fragile than we would
be if we were solitaries. As a member of a Catholic Worker
farm once put it: "Community means sharing a deep sense of
vulnerability. That's where grace comes in, when we are
wounded, we recognize our poverty, we get the grace to make
our wounds visible, to trust."[2]

If this isn't enough of a caution against thinking of community as some kind of hermetically sealed safety zone, here's
something else to chew on: community is also the place where
we can expect to suffer for the sake of others. Dorothy Day
once wrote that compassion—"suffering with" others—is the
foundation of community, and compassion always seeks to
both share and alleviate another's pain. Moreover, genuine
compassion extends far beyond the borders of one's immediate environment to reach out to the entire world's suffering.
When asked, "Who is my neighbor, who is a member of my
community?" Jesus matter-of-factly replied: "Everyone." And
that's the way it should be. "If we all carry a little of the
burden," Day wrote, "it will be lightened. If we share in the
suffering of the world, then some will not have to endure so
heavy an affliction. It evens out."[3]

The great difficulty is that our deep wound inhibits us from
treating one another as neighbors. In the last chapter we saw
how our fear of vulnerability causes us to see the temporal
world as an adversary to be seized and conquered. A similar

dynamic is at work when it comes to the way we see other humans. We look at them, and our insecurity pushes us to see not persons made in the likeness of God, but enemies—or at least threats—who must be defeated in order to gain what we desire or hold onto what we have.

This distrust of the other is found at every point along the social spectrum: governmental, social, local, individual. It reveals itself as ethnic hatred or religious dogmatism or regional chauvinism or economic inequality. Frequently, it comes across as sheer indifference. On the surface, the priest and the Levite in Jesus's parable of the good Samaritan appear not to help the wounded wayfarer because they just don't give a damn about his well-being. But indifference is usually a coverup. We *act* indifferent, but at a deeper level we are frightened. Our fear prods us into depersonalizing others, thus adopting an outward appearance of indifference, as a defense mechanism. Yet psychological defense mechanisms are never totally successful. Despite our show of indifference, we remain convinced that most people—all those "others" who inhabit the world alongside us—are threats to our well-being. We distrust because we fear.

Necessity is the mother of invention. The era in which we live has demonstrated a great deal of ingenuity in legitimizing our fear of the other. In the history of Western thought a few voices lament what they see as the wolfish tendencies of the human beast: Diogenes the Cynic, the author of Ecclesiastes, John Calvin, Thomas Hobbes, and Arthur Schopenhauer come immediately to mind. But until recently, this sentiment has been the minority opinion. Most past thinkers acknowl-edged that humans can act beastly but insisted that this unhappy tendency is learned rather than innate.[4] No more. The fashion these days is to insist that we are "naked apes," killers "red in tooth and claw" beneath our thin veneer of

civilization. Freud warns that the violent instincts of the
unconscious are always in danger of bursting forth in overt
behavior. Konrad Lorenz argues that *homo sapiens* is the only
species that regularly (and gleefully) kills members of its own
kind. Socio-biologists such as Richard Dawkins claim that
humans are selfish even at the genetic level. These and like-
minded intellectuals over the last century or so have canonized
the claim that human nature is basically aggressive and untrustworthy.[5] Given this bleak assessment, we would be foolish not
to fear one another.

On the one hand, this intellectual legitimation of our ancient
fear is wonderfully convenient. It provides us with justification
for doing what we, in our desperate need for invulnerability,
want to do anyway: keep others at arm's length. But on the
other hand, its convenience is outweighed by the damage it
does. For we are *not* naked apes, and viewing other persons
as apish adversaries not only harms them at their deepest core
but also woefully diminishes us as well. Our panicky need to
think of others as menaces is, in the most profound sense, a
fall from innocence, because it substitutes an unnatural and
ultimately destructive fear for the God-intended love that
should unify humans into community and promote individual
flourishing. In defining humans as innately untrustworthy, we
have sidelined what Thomas Merton called the deep reality of
"communion."

> The deepest level of communication is not
> communication, but communion. It is wordless. It
> is beyond words, and it is beyond speech, and it
> is beyond concept. Not that we discover a new
> unity. We discover an older unity. . . . We are
> already one. But we imagine that we are not.

What we have to recover is our original unity.
What we have to be is what we are.[6]

Strangers in an Estranged Land

Our denial of the "original unity" Merton speaks about—a
unity grounded in our common God-likeness—is chiefly
characterized by our freezing the other into a stranger: someone who is alien, menacingly different from me and mine. This
immediately raises two questions: How do we go about
estranging another? What does it mean to be a stranger?

The act of estranging another has as its goal the denial of
his or her personhood. The essence of seeing someone as a
menacing other is to disregard any commonly shared traits or
hopes or fears and instead to reframe the person exclusively as
an alien. This eliminates the possibility of embarrassing
twinges of fellow-feeling on our part that may get in the way
of our anxious need to be safe. How can we have any fellow-
feeling for an alien?

We can depersonalize the other in any number of ways, but
all of them involve establishing ourselves within a protective
enclave that defensively shuts out the other. Enclaves tend to
come in two varieties: they are either ruggedly individualistic or
mindlessly collectivistic. Chances are good that most of us
belong to both sorts, and that we move back and forth between them as occasion and need arise.

We in the United States in particular have grown up in an
ethos that lauds individualism. Our cultural heroes tend to be
loners who stalwartly walk their own path in defiance of
convention or authority. They demand the right to be different, to keep government off their backs, and to decide for
themselves what they will do in life. Our icons of individualism

run the gamut from John Wayne cowboy types—strong and fiercely independent—to Jackson Pollock types—lonely, buck-the-system geniuses. Whether we incline toward the one or the other is a matter of temperament and background, but most of us are attracted to some extent to the overall ideal of self-reliance they represent. Even those who claim to deplore the culture of individualism are probably more influenced by it than they know.

While it can't be denied that there is nobility in resisting mindless conformity, it is also the sad case that the ideal of rugged individualism is frequently just an excuse for a narcissism that takes the security and empowerment of the self as the primary goals of existence. Friedrich Nietzsche, for example, is notorious for his defense of the *übermensch*, the "blond beast" of the future who accepts no master save himself.[7] He usually contrasted his cold-bloodedly self-reliant individualists with what he disparagingly called "the herd": the mindless, bovine crowd that has no will power or discipline. In such comparisons it is inevitable that the blond beast comes off looking good. But when screened from the angle of precarity, Nietzsche's *übermensch* is an advanced case of insecurity panic. He so desperately needs to carve out a safe place for himself in the world that he makes his very existence a citadel. He is his own kingdom, and everyone else is an intruder.[8]

It is to be hoped that not too many of us see ourselves as blond beasts, but quite a few of us who incline toward individualism might well do so for reasons similar to Nietzsche's *übermensch*. The ancient wound ceaselessly warns that we must be on our guard, that we must carefully wall up our emotions and thoughts in protective layers of psychological insulation, all for the purpose of making sure that the self isn't damaged. For a narcissist-cum-individualist, there isn't room in the world for more than one ego. So the individualist system-atically begins to obliterate other egos by reducing them to strangers, less-than-fully-personal (because different) aliens. The individualist typically does this through the scorn and hatred bred by fear. "I've no time for you," the individualist in effect says to everyone else in the world. "You're either an obstacle to be removed or just another alien lump of matter cluttering up my landscape. Get lost. Go away. Scram."[9]

So much for the individualist's mode of freezing others into strangers. What about the collectivist?

Although our culture praises the rugged, stand-alone individualist, many of us also find great comfort in identifying with one group or another. Political party, civic organization, religious denomination: it makes little difference what collec-tive we belong to, just so long as we find one. As we saw in Chapter 1, immersing oneself in a collective is one of the ways we typically seek to escape our essential precarity. In numbers is strength.

The collective ought not to be confused with community, although it is common to identify the two. The collective is more akin to what Martin Luther King Jr. often referred to as a "broken community." A broken community is one whose dynamics are typically defined by a brutal power-brokering that separates "us," the members of the group, from "them," the non-group others. As a consequence, broken communities are always rigidly exclusionary, and the members of a collec-tive feel justified in "circling the wagons" against any and all outsiders. These "strangers" are often held in contempt, always in suspicion. Sometimes, sadly, they are also demonized and persecuted by the collective. This kind of demonization led King to argue that "the group, the tribe, the race, and the nation" that constitute a broken community "often sink to levels of barbarity unthinkable even among lower animals."[10]

But this us-against-them mentality doesn't mean that there are significant ties of loyalty and respect among members of a collectivist group. For the most part, the only bonds holding together members of the broken community are fear of insecurity and desire for power. Ironically, this combination makes for instability within the group. Ad hoc coalitions form as expediency dictates and easily break apart when the occasion that gave rise to them passes. Insiders are always at risk of finding themselves outsiders.

Whether estrangement is performed by the rugged individualist whose life has no room for anyone else or by a collectivist who sees outsiders as intrinsically contemptible, its primary goal is the depersonalization of the other. Leonardo Boff argues that persons (as distinct from nonsouled objects) are made in the likeness of God and hence reflect divine qualities. God is open to creation, sensitive to the genuine needs and concerns of humanity; God's openness is empathic, a compassionate suffering and rejoicing with our suffering and rejoicing; and God's empathy translates into availability on God's part, a rolling-up-the-sleeves willingness to lend help (the most obvious example of which is the Incarnation). It follows that a person is characterized by three relational qualities analogous to God's: an openness to others, a communal bond with others, and an availability to others.[11] One of the great mysteries taught by Christianity is that we become better *persons* in proportion to how *Godlike* we are. Imitating God's "personhood"—which is the ultimate model for our own—awakens our humanity.

But when we estrange others, we deny them their personhood. We refuse to accept them as creatures made in the likeness of God. We rebuff their openness, dismissing it as nosiness or, even worse, self-interested meddling; we refuse to acknowledge a common bond connecting them and us; and we wouldn't dream of going out of our way to be available to them. They are adversaries, aliens, strangers, faceless and anonymous others. To treat them as anything more is to put ourselves at risk, to invite them into our own high-walled safety zone, to hazard the scary business of love.[12]

Safety-minded individualists and collectivists who estrange others by denying them their personhood typically don't worry about the damage they inflict on those whom they reduce to the status of strangers. They are too concerned with their own security needs to worry about anyone else's. The entire world is seen through their own fear-centered perspective.

This security-conscious way of looking at the world is not only sinful in its treatment of other humans. It is also foolish from a practical perspective, because it can't offer the protection that individualists and collectivists hope it will. French philosopher Simone de Beauvoir pointed this out when she argued that our well-being is intimately connected with the well-being of those who surround us in both our immediate and not-so-immediate environment. If we are surrounded by individuals who are spiritually and morally mature, this increases our own chances of fulfillment, because we are part of a community that values and promotes the genuinely good life. By the same token, if we are surrounded by morally and spiritually stunted individuals, odds are good that we will be tainted by the poisonous environment in which we dwell.

Now, if we, or the group to which we belong, indulge in denying others their personhood, we damage ourselves as well as the others whom we are rejecting. We diminish our own likelihood of achieving fulfillment because we blight our landscape, filling it with strangers with whom we refuse to interact in any meaningful way. There is no opportunity for growth in self-awareness or compassion or love, because we have surrounded ourselves with anonymous aliens whom we won't allow to touch us in a person-to-person way. Our safety barriers have separated us from the very wellsprings that could renew us. We huddle in our enclave, imagining that our little patch of ground is the center of the universe, unaware that we have turned it into an arid, personless landscape.[13]

De Beauvoir's point is essentially an ecological one: since our environment helps shape who we are, we ought to be especially careful in our stewardship of it. And a major part of our environment is other persons. In reducing them to strangers, we exile ourselves to a land of estrangement that robs our own lives of promise and hope. We sell our birthright for a mess of pottage, and all because we won't face and heal the ancient wound.

From Estrangement to Hospitality

We have seen that the mutation of others into strangers consists in denying them personhood, and that we engage in the act of estrangement because of our ancient wound. We have also noted that in denying personhood to others, we proportionately diminish our own as well. Any destruction of relational possibilities in our environment can't but harm us.

There is no other spin to put on it: the destruction wrought by estrangement is contrary to the spirit of Christianity. Christ entered the world to retrieve us from our fall from personhood and to give us a new vision of how to be fully human. With the coming of Christ, God initiated a new level of relational intimacy with us, inviting us into a divine space laden with the promise of fulfillment. Put a slightly different way, the Incarnation invited us into God's home so that we might prosper from God's hospitality. Hospitality to outsiders, rather than the deliberate estrangement of them, is what God expects of us in turn. This requires that we renounce our enclave mentality and

embrace precarity. Hospitality, like any other act of love, is
dangerous.

Hospitality is a virtue recommended by both Jesus and his
apostles. The parable of the good Samaritan is a story about
hospitality (Lk 10:25-37), as is the parable of the prodigal son
(Lk 15:11-32). The two disciples on the road to Emmaus
recognize the risen Jesus only after they offer him hospitality
(Lk 24:35). Paul tells members of the early church to practice
hospitality (Rom 12:13) and so does the author of Hebrews
(Heb 13:2). Similarly, the author of 1 Peter insists that hospitality should be given without reservation (1 Pt 4:9). From
earliest times the eucharistic love feast, the center of Christian
worship, was considered a living symbol of God's hospitality to
humans as well as God's calling of humans to be hospitable to
one another. Moreover, it was understood that hospitality
extended beyond the Christian family to embrace nonbelievers
as well (cf. Gal 6:10; 1 Thess 3:12).

Today we tend to have a much more domesticated (and
proportionately impoverished) understanding of hospitality.
For many of us, hospitality consists in inviting friends and
family into our homes to share a meal or to celebrate a
festive occasion. The primary emphasis here is on "friends
and family." Hospitality, the invitation to cross the border that
separates our private enclave from the public domain, is
extended only to those whom we already know and trust.
Moreover, we tend to offer hospitality mainly to entertain or
amuse. Cocktail parties, dinner parties, birthday parties,
holiday parties: the key word here is apparent. Finally, our
hospitality is usually carefully choreographed: dinner menus
are planned far in advance, the house is scrubbed and
polished until everything is just so. We blanch at the prospect
of uninvited guests to whom we must offer spontaneous
hospitality.

But the ancient Christian notion of hospitality was quite
different. Those to whom hospitality was properly directed
were outsiders, not friends or family. Outsiders, then as now,
are strangers who, because of their very strangeness, are
frightening. In inviting these aliens into their personal, private
space, the early Christians in effect treated them as they would
family members. This all but forgotten meaning of hospitality—loving strangers as if they were members of one's own
household—is explicit in one of the Greek words for hospitality, *philoxenia*, a combination of *phileo* (kinship love) and
xenos (stranger).

Moreover, hospitality for the early Christian community
wasn't a matter of entertainment so much as care and nurtur-
ing. Even if entertainment was sometimes part of the particular hospitality extended to guests, it was never an essential
ingredient. In the main, hospitality was seen as a privileged
opportunity to offer sustenance and recuperation for the soul
as well as the body.

In addition, early Christians recognized that genuine hospitality was often required on the spur of the moment as unex-
pected travelers, weary from their journey, showed up on the
doorstep. Hospitality wasn't choreographed because it wasn't
seen as a set-aside, special occurrence. Making one's home
available to those in need of one was a normal part of everyday life.[14]

Actually, the word *home* is essential to appreciating the
ancient understanding of hospitality. To offer hospitality isn't
simply to *open* one's home to the stranger; it is to *offer* one's
home to the stranger, thereby treating the stranger as kin.
Philoxenia, the family love of strangers, replaces *xenophobia*,
the fear of them precisely and only because they *are* strangers.

Home immediately conjures up associations and images
quite different from those suggested by *safety zone, enclave,*

or *fortress.* These terms all imply fear, danger, tension. *Home,* on the other hand, has less aggressive, more intimate connotations. It suggests a place where love and mutual respect and trust abound, a place where personhood is possible. As Rosemary Haughton says, "Home is the place where I belong, and that belongs to me. It defines who I am. The image of home, the symbols and festivals and memories, assure me of who I am and give me a specific value."[15]

When genuine hospitality is extended—the kind of hospitality encouraged by Jesus and practiced by his first followers— we invite strangers to come and belong to a place that, for us, is redolent of goodness. We willingly break down the conventional barriers that separate the private from the public by transforming our private home into an open home. In offering real hospitality to others, we don't seek to co-opt them or to remake them in our own image. We *do* intend, however, to give them a place to which they can belong, and in belonging, discover who they are. Henri Nouwen puts this point nicely:

> The paradox of hospitality is that it wants to
> create an emptiness, not a fearful emptiness, but
> a friendly emptiness where strangers can enter
> and discover themselves as created free; free to
> sing their own songs, speak their own languages,
> dance their own dances; free also to leave and
> follow their own vocations. Hospitality is not a
> subtle invitation to adopt the lifestyle of the host,
> but the gift of a chance for the guest to find his
> own.[16]

Offering hospitality, in short, propels us out of the enclave mentality encouraged by our wounded anxiety and allows us to facilitate personhood in others instead of estranging them. In extending hospitality and thereby creating a space where others can come into their own, we also become fuller persons ourselves. In Parker Palmer's words, "Through the stranger our view of self, of world, of God is deepened and expanded. Through the stranger we are given a chance to find ourselves. And through the stranger, God finds us and offers us the gift of wholeness in the midst of our estranged lives, a gift of God and of the public life."[17] Just as we discover the Eternal in the passing moment when we open ourselves to the temporal order in which we exist, so we find the healing, renewing God in the stranger to whom we offer the gift of hospitality.

Hospitality is the key to moving beyond our individualistic or collectivistic fortresses and stepping out into the open. But precisely because of this, hospitality is also dangerous. Whenever we practice hospitality, we don't just fling our doors open to the unknown and the uncertain. We actively invite the unknown and the uncertain to cross our threshold so that we may trust and love them. Trust and love, as we have already seen, accentuate rather than downplay our vulnerability. But as we have also seen, this is the price we must pay for breathing fresh air and feeling the sun on our flesh. This is the price of relationship and personhood. And it is also the price if we wish to move from broken to genuine community.

The Beloved Community

Martin Luther King Jr. was interested in the broken community only insofar as it could shed light on its ideal counterpart, what he frequently called the "beloved community." The beloved community for King maximizes relationship and hence personhood, and in doing so models the deep interconnectedness of reality:

> In a sense all life is interrelated. All men and
> women are caught in an inescapable network of
> mutuality, tied in a single garment of destiny.
> Whatever affects one directly affects all indirectly.
> I can never be what I ought to be until you are
> what you ought to be, and you can never be what
> you ought to be until I am what I ought to be.
> This is the interrelated structure of reality.[18]

On a superficial level King's remark can be read as an expression of blatant self-interest: because my destiny is necessarily tied up with yours in a "network of mutuality," it is to my advantage to get along with you. But pacts based solely on self-interest never last very long. They are characteristic of broken communities, and we have already seen that expediency is the name of the game there.

More significantly, King's point is that we are necessarily related to one another because the "structure of reality," at its very core, is likewise "interrelated." The universe is one vast community, and the driving force behind its cohesion is love. As Eberhard Arnold wrote, "We must live in community because all life created by God exists in a communal order and works toward community."[19] To think of reality as a vast collection of only accidentally related individuals is to misunderstand its deep nature. There is a unity to it—Merton's "older unity" of communion—that suggests harmony and wholeness rather than division and solitariness. For both King and Arnold, this unity is a consequence of the divine Love that breathed the world into being and continues to sustain it.

Groping for a way to express the intuition that the universe is held together by God's creative love, the early Christians, inspired by Saint Paul, came up with the image of the mystical body of Christ. Members of the Christian community are related to one another as the cells and organs in a body are related. Each has its own specific task to perform, although each is still allowed a good deal of creative leeway. But the identity of each is defined through its incorporation into the whole, and the unity and harmony of the whole—the body's "health," to conclude the analogy—holds everything in place.

As creatures made in the likeness of God, endowed with an ability to love and nurture and commune analogous to God's, we are all inseparably connected both to God and to one another. We share the same lineage, the same spiritual blood type. Despite all our differences, we are essentially bound by divine love into a harmonious unity—the mystical body.

What this means, in turn, is that there really are no strangers, even though we try hard to invent them. Everyone we meet is a spiritual relative (God's kingdom is really a *kin*dom), linked to us by indissoluble love. When we gaze into the face of another, we should discover there a trinity of persons. We should see the other in all his or her palpable particularity; we should see an intimation of the God whose image that person is; and we should see a reflection of ourselves, our own hopes and fears and joys. When we embrace the other as a family member, we simply acknowledge the "older unity" that ties creation together.

I use the expression "gaze into the face of another" deliberately in order to underscore the importance of personal flesh-and-blood encounters for the growth of the beloved community. Securely ensconced in our enclaves, we seldom see the faces of those we dismiss as strangers. Instead, one of two things generally happens. Either strangers are freeze-dried into anonymous and non-threatening abstractions, or they are demonized as horrendous threats that call for the buttressing of safety zones. Both of these strategies of depersonalizing strangers have been applied recently, for example, to Muslim fundamentalists. Prior to 9/11, our usual way of thinking about them was statistical: so many of them, from such-and-such demographic groups, live "over there" somewhere in the Middle East. Since 9/11, we have switched to strategies of demonization: all Muslim fundamentalists are mad-dog terrorists consumed with the lust to wash their hands in infidel blood. Both of these approaches sacrifice the real person for a lifeless equation, on the one hand, or a Hollywoodish caricature, on the other, thereby eroding the possibility of communication, much less the deeper communion about which Thomas Merton writes.

In order to relate to strangers as kin, we must come into personal contact with them as they are, not as we wish or fear them to be. A concrete encounter between real flesh-and-blood persons is the only way to see faces behind the masks we impose on others. Without such encounters we have no incentive to think of strangers as anything but threats. Doubting Thomas, who has generally gotten a bad rap in Christian tradition, was wise enough to know this. When he demanded to see the risen Christ—and not just to see him but actually to finger his wounds, the undeniable marks of Christ's realness—Thomas stubbornly witnessed to the importance of gazing into the other's face and touching the other's flesh.

The beloved community is founded on such encounters as this, and a first step in the building of that community is to make ourselves available to strangers in acts of hospitality. When we invite strangers into our private places, rather than scurrying to keep them on the other side of our security barriers, we can get a good, long look at their faces. Then we see into their souls and know that we stand in the presence of *persons* with whom, because of our common origin, we are deeply kindred.

But as we have noted, this recognition always entails risk, because it always means leaving our safety zone, venturing into the open, unprotected space of communion, and suffering alongside the beloved when he or she is in pain. So if the beloved community is a modeling of the deeper connectedness that permeates the universe, then it stands to reason that risk is woven into the very fabric of creation. God takes a risk in creating us, because it is quite possible that we might refuse to reciprocate God's generous hospitality; we take a risk when-ever we open our hearts and homes to an other—including God—because doing so means, at the very least, that we will be called upon to hazard the pain of rejection or the distress of empathic suffering. Yet this riskiness—this *precarity*—is simply unavoidable. It comes with communion. We can't have one without the other. Communion takes place in the shadow of the cross.

When we finally realize this, we free ourselves to accept others as the persons they are, not the threatening strangers our ancient wound makes them out to be. This re-awakening to the splendor in others, a splendor in which we ourselves participate, is in turn the impetus we need to begin actively collaborating with God to repair the broken communities in which we currently dwell and turn them into the beloved communities they are meant to be. Communion is never passive (yet another reason why it's risky). Communion is in the dangerous but exhilarating business of fixing what is broken and revitalizing what is moribund—which means, for King, that communion is really an expression of love, "the only cement that can hold the broken community together. When I am commanded to love, I am commanded to restore community, to resist injustice, and to meet the needs of my brothers and sisters."[20]

In building the beloved community, resisting injustice, and helping all humans to flourish, we are called not to overcome but to embrace insecurity, to wield power by forsaking power, and to put ourselves in danger for the sake of loving others into unbroken communion and full being. We are called, in short, to put our money where our mouths are, and this, as we will discover in the next chapter, means following the path of downward mobility toward an ever bolder embrace of precarity.

◄ 4 ►

Taking the Downward Path

*My power is made perfect
in weakness.*
—2 Cor 12:8

The Same Old Same-Old

A mantra has seized our imagination since the 9/11 terrorist attacks: Things will never be the same again. We hear it chanted everywhere: at family get-togethers, lines at bus stops, in the media, from pulpits in churches, temples, and mosques. You've probably said it yourself. I know I have.

In the most obvious sense, what we mean when we lament that things are forever changed is that our longstanding confidence in our own untouchability has been badly damaged. We now know that we are vulnerable, that we can be hurt and even killed on our own soil. Equally disturbing is the loss of our rather naive and perhaps overly self-satisfied confidence that the world's inhabitants fondly (even if a bit enviously) think of us as a benevolent big brother. We are now all too dreadfully aware that millions of people despise us. The airliners that smashed into building and earth on 9/11 likewise smashed these two myths, leaving us with the anxious fear that things will never be the same again.[1]

But while some things *do* seem changed, many others are
the same. Dentists still drill cavities, pubs still hold happy
hours, utility bills still come in the mail. You and I continue to
go about our daily chores. Old routines, temporarily disrupted
by the horror of 9/11, have recommenced. Life goes on, even
when we feel it somehow ought not.

Part of the reason for this resumption of the normal is the
amazing resilience of human beings. We bounce back after
disasters, tighten our belts, and rebuild what was destroyed.
Communities and individuals, around the world and throughout history, time and again have demonstrated this resolve to
begin anew. It is one of our more admirable traits—one of our
more "handsome conditions," as Ralph Waldo Emerson would
say. We witnessed moving displays of such courageous resilience in the days following 9/11, when firemen, cops, and
disaster, construction, and medical teams from all over the
country unstintingly threw themselves into rescue work in
Manhattan.[2]

But there is also another, less handsome reason why many
things have remained the same: the stubborn refusal to take
advantage of the opportunities for self-examination and
growth provided by the 9/11 limit situation. This resistance
doubtless has many causes, with old-fashioned inertia surely
being one of them. But, as I have argued throughout, the
deepest cause is our primordial fear of insecurity. Change and
novelty are usually frightening (even if sometimes pleasurably,
excitingly so) because they push us from the known into the
unknown. Crises such as the terrorist attacks may call our old
ways of doing things and interpreting the world into question,
raising the distressing possibility that things need to change.
But our wounded fear of risk resists this possibility, and we
scramble to reestablish the status quo as soon as the immediate threat passes. No matter that the status quo may not

actually be all that desirable. It is what we know and what we feel safe in.

A couple of things that have stayed very much the same is our obsession with national security and the attendant conviction that the only way to achieve safety is through force of arms. If anything, in fact, they have become even more canonical since 9/11. The United States government has launched a worldwide, long-term war against terrorism, calling up troops and pulling out the latest war machines from the Pentagon's astoundingly sophisticated arsenal. In declaring the war shortly after 9/11, President Bush drew a clear line in the sand, telling the world's nations that if they chose not to join in, they were expected at least to step aside and not interfere. But he also made it clear that the United States would remember those who refused to take part, suggesting that neutrality in the face of a global threat to civilization (as the 9/11 assault was called) was a betrayal. Nothing less than the survival of the nation and the security of the global community were at stake, so anything less than a swift and sure military response was inappropriate.

Clearly, many people in the United States share the administration's conviction that a violent retaliation to the 9/11 assaults, as well as "proactive" violence to forestall future ones, is appropriate—so much so, in fact, that dissenting voices are greeted with astonishment and outrage. The panicked fury felt by my church lady and millions more like her broke out in particularly bellicose language immediately after 9/11. Historian and journalist Paul Johnson, for example, wrote that "it is vitally important that America stick to the essentials of its military response and carry it through relentlessly and thoroughly." Writing in *Time* magazine, Lance Morrow argued that "America needs to relearn a lost discipline, self-confident relentlessness—and to relearn why human nature has equipped us all with a weapon (abhorred in decent peacetime societies) called hatred." Orthodox rabbi Daniel Lapin opined that terrorists ought to be exterminated in the methodically brutal way the ancient Hebrews wiped out the Amalekites.[3]

Now, some months after the terrorist attacks, with the Taliban destroyed and al-Qaeda's Afghanistan-based network severely damaged, cries for military retaliation are a bit more temperate. But the conviction remains that national security warrants a continuation of violence until terrorism is utterly wiped out. In fact, national righteousness demands it. This position has been most ably expressed by William Bennett in his recent *Why We Fight,* a defense of the U.S. war against terrorism.[4]

Bennett's starting point is that our "postmodern culture" has fallen into murky confusion when it comes to values and moral decision-making. We lean, he claims, toward a norma-tive relativism that recognizes no ethical standards other than the rather unpredictable fashions of time and place. No action or character trait is good or evil in itself (even using traditional normative terms such as these is hard for the postmodernist). Moral value is determined exclusively by context. And since contexts continuously shift, so do values, leaving us either bewildered or cynical when it comes to ethics.

But if there was ever an event that swept away postmodern hair-splitting and created occasion for what Bennett calls "moral clarity," it was 9/11. In the destruction of the World Trade Towers, the attack on the Pentagon, and the crash of the fourth hijacked airliner in Pennsylvania, the world wit-nessed acts that no rational person could evaluate in any other way but terribly, horrendously evil. Moreover, the appropriate moral response to the attacks is also transparently obvious: "Retaliation [should] be swift and uncompromising, adequate to the outrage, and in keeping with the dictates of our moral and political traditions."[5] What could be more obvious?

Yet there were and are some in this country—mainly intellectuals, says Bennett—whose postmodern myopia prevents them from seeing the moral clarity offered by the events of 9/11. Even if they are willing to concede his first point—that the terrorist assault is obviously evil—they resist his second—that violence is the morally appropriate response to such evil. Such dissenters cast "a shadow of moral doubt over our righteous and justified anger," thereby weakening national resolve and damaging national security.[6] Bennett asks:

> But why must we accept [their] premise that anger is itself a suspect quality and always in need of "management"? To the contrary, as the ancients recognized, anger is a necessary power of the soul, intimately connected with the passion for justice. The appeal to stifle our anger and negotiate our differences with extremists bent on nullifying our existence [is] thus not only irrelevant, it [is] immoral; it amount[s] to a counsel of unilateral disarmament and a denial of justice.[7]

Note what is going on here. Bennett, like so many of us, is thinking in a very conventional mode indeed, and that mode is one of the things that 9/11 appears not to have changed much at all. He assumes that the only way "righteous anger" can properly respond to violence is through still more violence, and that disagreement with this strategy amounts to a "denial of justice" (as well as being foolishly suicidal). In mechanically associating anger and violence, he conflates the two in a way that Christians, if we truly follow the example

and words of Christ, must find unacceptable. Moral clarity
about 9/11 does indeed call for anger. But the "management"
of anger decried by Bennett doesn't question the virtue of
righteous anger so much as the ways in which that anger
should be expressed. Christ, after all, was angry on several
occasions, especially when he witnessed cruelty or injustice or
indifference to suffering. But he taught that nonviolent ways of
acting out the anger must be sought.

The point is that one of the things *not* changed forever by
9/11 is our conventional way of dealing with threats to our
safety. Our ancient wound continues to push us into response
modes of power-brokering, saber-rattling, and war, modes that
are as ancient as the wound itself. Our anxious sense of
vulnerability causes us to fear, estrange, and despise whoever
threatens or harms us and then to lash out at them in panic
and fury, all the while claiming that we are only doing what
the moral demands of "righteous anger" require. This dynamic
is all too observable at both the personal and national level,
and it is born from our deeply rooted fear of insecurity.
Whether it's the raised middle finger of a respectable church
lady or the more sophisticated analysis of William Bennett, the
response is just more of the same old same-old. Things most
definitely haven't changed forever—not yet, anyway.

I mentioned in the Introduction that 9/11, like any limit
situation, offers opportunities for reflection and insight into
how we live and how we ought to live. Previous chapters have
explored several of those opportunities: embracing rather than
fleeing our poverty and provisionality, celebrating the temporal
order in which we live as a vehicle for the eternal, recognizing
and communing with others as persons rather than rejecting
them as strangers. In this final chapter, I explore one more
opportunity offered by 9/11, an opportunity that, in a fundamental way, is the culmination of all the others. It is the

opportunity to turn away from our wounded guns-and-fists mode of responding to threats to our safety long enough to consider an alternative that, in keeping with Christ's message, focuses on reconciliation and peace. This way acknowledges our essential vulnerability without trying to whitewash the fearsomeness of it. But at the same time, it refuses to be goaded into the destructiveness—the *sinfulness*—of blind fear or "unmanaged" anger.

High Road, Low Road

One way to begin understanding the new opportunity offered us by 9/11 is to think about it in terms of the distinction between upward and downward mobility that Henri Nouwen explored in several of his books.

Nouwen believes we live in a culture whose chief standard of success is upward mobility: the frenetic and utterly self-absorbed scramble to scratch and claw one's way to the top of the food chain. The supreme values of an ethos of upward mobility are strength, efficiency, and success. *Excellence* is one of its favorite buzzwords, a euphemism that basically signifies coming out on top at any price. A person or nation striving for "excellence" is properly contemptuous of weakness, indifferent to the needs of others, and suspicious of friendly overtures from strangers. People are viewed as leeches, competitors or aggressors, or (at best) temporary allies to be discarded as soon as their usefulness is exhausted. The only thing that really matters to the upwardly mobile climber is power: power to dominate others, to be feared by others, to be untouchable by the assaults of others.

The portrait of upward mobility painted by Nouwen is painfully familiar. Upwardness permeates our way of living, our value system, and the standards by which we gauge success and failure. Sometimes it expresses itself in crass terms of vaunting ambition, but just as frequently it masks itself in the high tones of duty. "My whole life I have been sur- rounded by well-meaning encouragement to go 'higher up,'" comments Nouwen, "and the most-used argument was: 'You can do so much good there, for so many people.'"[8]

Why do so many of us give and receive encouragement to go "higher up"? To account for upward mobility merely by invoking social conditioning is too simplistic, because such a solution begs the question of its origin. So we must probe more deeply: what is there about the human condition that seeds the lust for power characteristic of upward mobility?

Nouwen approaches this question by appealing to the story of Jesus' three wilderness temptations:

> The "Tempter" came to him asking him to prove that he was worth being loved. The "Tempter" said to him: "Do something useful, like turning stones into bread. Do something sensational, like throwing yourself down from a high tower. Do something that brings you power, like paying me homage." These three temptations were three ways to seduce Jesus into becoming a competitor for love. The world of the "Tempter" is precisely that world in which people compete for love through doing useful, sensational, and powerful things and so winning medals that gain them affection and admiration.[9]

This is a remarkable insight into the deep psychology of upward mobility. Nouwen's point is that the lust for power comes not from hubris or arrogant ambition—these are symptoms, not causes—but instead from the heart-sickening

fear of not being loved. In fighting their way to the top,
upwardly mobile climbers hope to do something so useful, so
powerful, so sensational, that people will be bound to notice
and admire them. Love is what they want, but they are so
forlorn and lonely that they will settle for mere attention.
Pathetically, they may even confuse the two. Since the world
teaches that everyone must compete for attention (as Andy
Warhol famously quipped, everyone's entitled to only fifteen
minutes of fame), upwardly mobile achievers conclude that
love is a limited resource that must be competed for as well.
Until they win the love they crave, until they feel safely loved
by others (even if, in their brokenness, they mistake notoriety
or publicity for genuine love), they suffer from an (at best)
nagging sense of anxiety.

Nouwen's insight helps us better understand the ancient
wound that draws us toward worldly empowerment and safety
spiritualities. We now see that our deeply rooted fear of
insecurity is actually the consequence of an even deeper need
to be loved. If we feel unloved, we quake with the dreadful
sense of insecurity that afflicts an orphaned or abused child
and search for ways to make ourselves less vulnerable. The
tragedy, as we have seen, is that the upwardly mobile way of
pursuing safety only aggravates our anxiety. Security barriers—money, social prestige, political clout—just give us
something else to worry about: will they endure? Frantic
struggles to freeze time only accentuate the speed with which
it slips through our fingers. Consolidating personal power by
transforming everyone else into strangers exiles us from
genuine community and ratchets up our terrible loneliness.
And celebrities can all painfully testify to the fact that fifteen
minutes of fame don't add up to love.

The upward path, then, won't give us what we want (and,
more important, what we need): love. This leaves us with the

lower path, the one that leads away from success and notoriety and power. Nouwen tells us that this second route, the one
of downward mobility, is "the descending way of Jesus. It is
the way toward the poor, the suffering, the marginal, the
prisoners, the refugees, the lonely, the hungry, the dying, the
tortured, the homeless."[10] The downward path, which commands us to leave our egos and our carefully contrived defense
strategies by the roadside, takes us straight to the place we
most resist going: the margins, the outback, the open spaces
of *ptoches* and provisionality, of precarity. It is God's invitation to us to join in the lovingly sacrificial way of the cross.
And as we saw in Chapter 1, it's precisely there that we find
God and come to realize that precarity doesn't mean only
"risk." It also signifies "dependence"—as Nouwen puts it,
"total and unconditional dependence on God that opens us to
be true channels of the divine power that heals."[11]

Just as upward mobility is the way of the world, so downward mobility goes against the world's grain. "Downward
mobility with Jesus," cautions Nouwen, "goes radically against
my inclinations, against the advice of the world surrounding
me, and against the culture of which I am a part."[12] That's
why, as we have already noted, divine grace is necessary to
nudge us in its direction. But when we finally (even if only
reluctantly) arrive at the place of marginality to which we are
called, the scales drop from our eyes and we are granted two
insights that liberate us—not from *insecurity*, mind you, but
from our obsessive need to *flee* from it.

The first and greatest insight is this: We are already loved.
Jesus was able to resist the "Tempter" because he didn't need
to prove to himself that he was worthy of love. He knew he
was *already* loved by God. Similarly, God has already and
always loved *us*. God loved us into being in the first place.
God's love sustains us throughout our existence, regardless of

how lost in forgetfulness and fear and upward mobility we might become. In loving us, God becomes radically vulnerable, because love is always risky. God surrenders the divine self-sufficiency for the sake of giving personhood to us and, in the process, growing from a relationship with us. This assumption of radical vulnerability on God's part is why we find God when we allow ourselves to enter into precarity and embrace rather than deny our ancient wound. Like recognizes like.

The second insight is this: Being loved by God doesn't mean that we are magically made safe and secure. Being loved is just as risky as loving. When it dawns on us that we are lovable (because God loves us), we also realize that God loves us because we are made in the supremely loving and lovable God's likeness. This, in turn, pushes us toward the discovery that, like the God on whom we are modeled, our nature is to reciprocate love, and that our hearts are restless until we do. Knowing that we are loved, then, necessarily leads to risking love ourselves, and this means living our vulnerability in an honest and straightforward manner. We will still be anxious about our radical exposure, and occasionally—particularly in times of crisis—find ourselves longing for safety zones and security barriers. How could we not? But we can live with the anxiety, because we are loved. And since God's judgment is trustworthy, we can *know*, as Jesus knew, that we are worthy of love. Being loved by God is the only assurance we need that we are indeed lovable.

Peacemaking

Nouwen concedes that many of us—perhaps most of us at one point or another in our lives—find the upward path's "temptation of power" well-nigh irresistible. Power, he speculates, "offers an easy substitute for the hard task of love. It seems

easier to be God than to love God, easier to control people
than to love people, easier to own life than to love life."[13]
We've already seen why love is a "hard task." It involves
putting ourselves at risk by leaving safety zones and venturing
out onto the margins.

The downward path, on the other hand, is more concerned
with peacemaking than power-brokering. Individuals—or
nations of individuals—who know that they are loved no
longer have to strut their egos in order to buy attention. Nor
are they so tortured by the ancient wound that they feel the
need to erect impregnable fortresses. Comfortable in their
awareness that the love they have been given is worth the
insecurity it brings, they are content to relate to their fellow
humans at the exact place where they find God: "not at the
apex of the pyramid of power, but at its base."[14]

It is clear that the downward path has no use for the worldly
mania for strength and security, and hence resists the temptation of power better than the upward path. But how does its
rejection of power-brokering translate into peacemaking?
Peacemaking implies overt activity in the world rather than a
private spirituality in which we mind our own business and
cultivate our own garden. So downward mobility isn't a meek
and mild withdrawal from the world, even though this is how it
is frequently interpreted. But why not?

The answer to this question must be sought in our recognition that we are worthy of love because God loves us. Once
we arrive at this insight—and, just as important, once we
manage to believe and accept it—we are not only liberated
from our own fearful sense of unworthiness. We're also freed
from our contemptuous tendency to see everyone else in the
world as unlovable. This, after all, is the crux of our freezing
others into strangers; if we loved them, they wouldn't be
strangers. A stranger isn't merely someone we don't know; he

or she is someone we don't think is worthy of love. But the moment we know ourselves to be loved, consistency compels us to acknowledge that all humans must be as lovable as we ourselves are, because they too were loved into being by God and made in the likeness of a loving and lovable God. If God finds them lovable, who are we to disagree?

Moreover, we begin to recognize that it is not just other humans who are lovable, because loved by God, but all of creation itself. Genesis tells us that after each day's work, God looked at what God had wrought and named it *tov*, or "good." To designate something as good is to say that it is desirable, admirable, love-worthy. The world, then, and all the creatures that dwell within it, are loved into being by God and sustained in their being by God's love.

Knowing that we as individuals are loved leads to the encompassing recognition that *nothing* created by God is unlovable. Everything is intrinsically worthy of our love and care and commitment. Moreover, because everything is kindred, bound by indissoluble ties of lovability, all of creation is necessarily influenced by what we do as well as what we don't do. Vietnamese Buddhist monk Thich Nhat Hanh reminds us that we are not "beings," stand-alone, self-sufficient entities. We are "interbeings," co-existing and hence co-depending on one another. "To be," writes Nhat Hanh, "is to inter-be. We cannot just be by ourselves alone. We have to inter-be with every other thing." And to inter-be with every other thing means that "we are responsible for everything that happens around us."[15]

Acceptance of our vulnerability for the sake of love; recognition that everything which exists, including myself, is worthy of love because loved by God; and acceptance of responsibility for the welfare of everything that inter-is—this is the potent combination that leads to peacemaking. For it is obvious that the only sane method of comporting ourselves in the world is serving that which is love-worthy and helping it to flourish. And if all creation is love-worthy, then this demands both personal actions and national policies that maximize the flourishing of creation. A violent rupture of the human and natural environments *never*, not even in the long run, contributes to their flourishing. Violence is always a break in the web of love that connects everything because violence is never a manifestation of love. Even worse, violence constitutes an assault on God, who is Love and who grounds love. As Walter Wink perceptively writes, "Christians are to be nonviolent, not simply because it 'works,' but because it reflects the very nature of God (Mt 5:45; Lk 6:35). Nonviolence is not a fringe concern. It is the very essence of the gospel."[16]

That many of us—even those who call ourselves Christian—disagree with this point testifies to the cultural prevalence of what Wink calls the "myth of redemptive violence." This is the claim that sometimes only violence is powerful enough to rescue order from chaos, and that in so doing violence redeems itself. But Wink dismisses this as a deceptive "ideology of conquest" that seeks moral justification for taking the easy way of violence instead of the harder way of peace and reconciliation. As I have argued in this book, there is also another explanation for why so many of us buy into the myth of redemptive violence. It helps us legitimate our wounded need to circle the wagons, build fortresses, and adopt a belligerent but self-righteous tone when we feel our safety is threatened. This, of course, only takes us back to Nouwen's central insight into the psychology of upward mobility: we generally crave power not because we're bastards but because we're so very frightened. But regardless of the reasons for indulging in it, violence, as Wink says, not only doesn't work, but it also damages the deep structure of creation and wounds the deep heart of God.

Breathing Space, Birthing Place

The downwardly mobile path, the path that Jesus took and commands us to take, is uniquely suited to peacemaking because it provides us with that opening in the otherwise tangled forest of fear and insecurity that Rowan Williams calls a "breathing space."[17] Without such breathing spaces, it is unlikely we could ever break free of the myth of redemptive violence. Our fear of insecurity would be too overwhelming to resist.

At the simplest level, a breathing space is a cooling-off period, an opportunity to calm down, take perspective, reflect on a given situation, weigh its wider implications, and only then reflectively and compassionately choose a course of responsive action. Jesus himself clearly appreciated the value of breathing space. When asked to comment on the woman taken in adultery, he responded to the furious, stone-in-fist crowd by silently drawing figures in the sand. Only after a few moments of this curious exercise did he speak. This is a strange deed that over the centuries has provoked speculation among the more gullible about magical signs and symbols. But in fact one of the things Jesus was doing was creating a breathing space; by deflecting the crowd's attention away from the adulterous woman to his scribbles in the sand, Jesus was giving the would-be executioners a much needed time-out. Only then were they calm enough for words of wisdom— Jesus' or anyone else's—to make a difference. A breathing space is an open space into which new perspectives can enter.

And what were the words that Jesus offered? Precisely the
message of downward mobility, the message of peacemaking.
We are all sinners, he told them, each and every one of us,
and therefore no one is qualified to act as this woman's holier-
than-thou judge. Look upon her with love and compassion,
because she is one of you; in fact, we are all interconnected by
bonds of love and lovability. You don't need to prove your
worth to God by stoning her in obedience to the law. God
already knows how worthy you are—you *and* this woman. Go
in peace, and try to love one another—that is, don't sin
anymore.

Downward mobility, since it devalues egoism and power-
brokering, allows us a respite from our usual need to be strong
and ruthless. The breathing space it affords is a genuine
opportunity for "moral clarity," for clarity is possible only
when our hearts and minds aren't clouded by anxiety or panic.
The person who chooses the downward path toward precarity
is no longer "puppet-stringed" by the ancient wound and is
able to respond in non-defensive ways to trying or dangerous
situations.

A breathing space, in other words, is the freedom to react
lovingly rather than fearfully and violently, to break the cycle
of offense, retaliation, and escalation. It liberates us, as
Williams says, to *choose* how we will respond to threats to our
security. And as Jesus knew when he confronted the blood-
thirsty crowd, freedom from fear is a great incentive to stop
hating the other. Once we acknowledge and use the breathing
space provided by downward mobility, then,

> it ought to be less likely that we reach for vio-
> lence as a first resort. We have the freedom to
> think what we actually want, to probe our desires
> for some kind of outcome that is more than just

mirroring what we have experienced. The trouble
is that this means work of the kind we are often
least eager for, work that will help us so to
understand an other that we begin to find some
sense of what they and we together might
recognize as good. It means putting on hold our
most immediate feelings—or at least making
them objects of reflection; it means trying to pull
apart the longing to re-establish the sense of
being in control and the longing to find a security
that is shared. . . . It is about trying to act so that
something might possibly change, as opposed to
acting so as to persuade ourselves that we're not
powerless.[18]

The freedom breathing space gives us to be morally clear—
to reflect on what the loving response to an interconnected
and ultimately lovable world ought to be—doesn't mean, of
course, that crises such as 9/11 won't cause us fear and
anger. Nor does it mean that we will refrain from morally
condemning violent acts perpetrated by others. Any violation
of the beloved community should call us forth as prophets. But
it does mean that we will "manage" our anger, to invoke the
expression used by William Bennett, making sure that it
doesn't explode into a return of violence for violence, doing
our best to resist allowing the anger to push us into frightened
modes of estranging others and enclaving ourselves, channel-
ing the anger's energy toward justice and reconciliation. And
when we do this, we discover that the breathing space is also a
birthing place that nurtures renewal of both ourselves and our
sisters and brothers. Breathing space, in other words, is that
liminal area between our old, anxiety-ridden longing for
untouchability and our transfigurative acceptance of ourselves

and everyone else, as loved, loving, and vulnerable. As such, it is a threshold to the kingdom—the kindom—of God.

Return to the Jabbok

Early in this book I retold the story of Jacob the Grabber's anxious return to the land of his fathers and mothers. He came home after many years' absence, richer but not much wiser. He originally fled his native land because his obsessive need for security had caused him to cheat his brother and lie to his aged father. He returned because the same need pushed him into stealing from his father- and brothers-in-law. Jacob's youthful upward mobility made things too hot for him at home, his middle-aged upward mobility made things too hot in his adopted land. Rather pitiful, when you think about it, but not unlike many of us.

And then the mysterious assailant attacked him on the bank of the Jabbok River. The stranger wounded Jacob, and in wounding him blessed him, and in blessing him changed his name and his life.

We are now better able to appreciate the full significance of Jacob's wrestling match that fateful night at the Jabbok. I don't think it is too much to say that one way of thinking about what happened is to see Jacob's assailant as Jacob himself. Here is a man who has spent his entire life hurting people because he feels unworthy of love and terribly lonely and scared as a consequence. He sits on that forlorn river-bank, squinting into the darkness in hope of catching a glimpse of his homeland, and it suddenly dawns on him that he has no homeland. His frenzy to deny his poverty and provisionality has exiled him from the home of his father and mother; his mania for seizing the day and making it his own has made him restless and dissatisfied; and his frightened habit of freezing everyone into strangers has left him without a single ally in the entire world.

As he sat there, regretting the past and fearing the future, the futility and misery of his safety-zoned life must have hit him so hard that it knocked the wind right out of him. Then the famous wrestling match began. For the entire night, Jacob fought with the fear and anxiety and lovelessness that had tortured him ever since he was a boy. The struggle revealed to him the ancient wound, and for the first time he steeled himself to face its hurt honestly and straightforwardly. By the time morning came, he was exhausted, haunted by what he had learned about himself, forever scarred by the struggle. But he was also blessed by the hard-won insight that vulnerability is the human condition precisely because it is God's condition, and that without it we can experience none of the joy and fulfillment intended for us.

Jacob probably thought back to his flight from home so many years ago, when he had slept fitfully in the desert, dreamed of a wondrous ladder stretching up to heaven, and awoke the next morning with the startled realization that God had been even there, in the wasteland, on the margins, out in the unprotected openness of the desert, all the time.

A good lesson for those of us who long for safety and security to take to heart.

Notes

Introduction: Wrestling with Vulnerability

1. Stratford Caldecott, "War without Boundaries," in *Beauty for Ashes: Spiritual Reflections on the Attack on America*, ed. John Farina (New York: Crossroad, 2001), 228-29.

2. Martin L. Smith, *Reconciliation* (Boston: Cowley, 1985), 80.

3. William T. Cavanaugh, "Faith Fires Back: A Conversation with Stanley Hauerwas," *Duke Magazine* (January-February 2002), 12.

4. Walter Brueggemann, *Praying the Psalms* (Winona, Minn.: Christian Brothers, 1993), 14.

5. Ralph Waldo Emerson, "Circles," in *The Portable Emerson*, ed. Carl Bode (New York: Penguin, 1981), 239.

6. Eugene Peterson, *Under the Unpredictable Plant: An Exploration in Vocational Holiness* (Grand Rapids, Mich.: Eerdmans, 1992), 68.

7. Marie Dennis, Joseph Nangle, O.F.M., Cynthia Moe-Lobeda, and Stuart Taylor, *St. Francis and the Foolishness of God* (Maryknoll, N.Y.: Orbis Books, 2000), 36.

1. Beyond Barriers

1. Sigmund Freud, *The Future of an Illusion*, trans. W. D. Robson-Scott and James Strachey (Garden City, N.J.: Anchor Books, 1964), 18-28.

2. Richard Geldard, *The Vision of Emerson* (Rockport, Mass.: Element, 1995), 21.

3. Michael Ramsey, quoted in George Appleton, "Praying for Peace," in *Peace Together: A Vision of Christian Pacifism*, ed. Clive Barrett (Cambridge: James Clarke & Co., 1987), 43.

4. Lucien Richard, O.M.I., *Living the Hospitality of God* (New York: Paulist Press, 2000), 19.

5. Bruce Wilkinson, *The Prayer of Jabez: Breaking through to the Blessed Life* (Sisters, Oreg.: Multnomah Publishers, 2000), 92, italics added.

6. Ibid., 31.

7. John Ferguson, "The Biblical Basis of Pacifism," in Barrett, *Peace Together*, 21.

8. C. S. Lewis, *A Grief Observed* (New York: Bantam, 1980), 77, 83.

9. John Dear, *Living Peace: A Spirituality of Contemplation and Action* (New York: Doubleday, 2001), 39-40.

10. Dorothy Day, "Poverty and Precarity," in *Dorothy Day: Selected Writings,* ed. Robert Ellsberg (Maryknoll, N.Y.: Orbis Books, 1992), 107.

11. Johannes B. Metz, *Poverty of Spirit*, trans. John Drury (New York: Paulist Press, 1968), 40.

12. John Farina, ed., *Beauty for Ashes: Spiritual Reflections on the Attack on America* (New York: Crossroad, 2001), 269.

13. John Main, *Word into Silence* (New York: Paulist Press, 1981), 59.

14. Oscar Romero, quoted in Marie Dennis, Renny Golden, and Scott Wright, *Oscar Romero: Reflections on His Life and Writings* (Maryknoll, N.Y.: Orbis Books, 2000), 28.

15. Karl Rahner, *Theological Investigations* 20 (New York: Crossroad/Herder & Herder, 1981), 175.

16. Alan Watts, *The Wisdom of Insecurity* (New York: Vintage, 1968), 27.

17. Metz, *Poverty of Spirit*, 41.

18. Richard Rohr and Joseph Martos, *The Great Themes of Scripture: Old Testament* (Cincinnati, Ohio: St. Anthony Messenger Press, 1987), 13.

19. Stanley Hauerwas and William H. Willimon, *Resident Aliens: Life in the Christian Colony* (Nashville, Tenn.: Abingdon Press, 1989), 88.

20. John Macquarrie, *Christology Revisited* (Harrisburg, Pa.: Trinity Press International, 1998), 38-39.

21. Dorothy Day, "The Pearl of Great Price," in Ellsberg, *Dorothy Day,* 113.

2. Seeing and Thanking

1. Martin Heidegger, *What Is Called Thinking?*, trans. J. Glenn Gray (New York: HarperCollins, 1976), 138-43.

2. Horace, "Ode 1," trans. Edwin Arlington Robinson, in *Latin Poetry*, ed. L. R. Lind (Boston: Houghton Mifflin, 1957), 102.

3. For a frightening study of our obsessive need to be entertained, see Neil Postman, *Amusing Ourselves to Death: Public Discourse in the Age of Show Business* (New York: Vintage, 1986).

4. I've discussed the length to which we go to attain the illusion of power in *Godlust: Facing the Demonic, Embracing the Divine* (New York: Paulist Press, 1999).

5. Kerry Walters, ed., *Rufus Jones: Essential Writings* (Maryknoll, N.Y.: Orbis Books, 2001), 81-82.

6. Annie Dillard, *Pilgrim at Tinker Creek* (New York: HarperCollins, 1974), 81.

7. Ibid.

8. Walters, *Rufus Jones,* 42.

9. Dillard, *Pilgrim at Tinker Creek*, 79.

10. Gregory of Nyssa, *The Lord's Prayer*, trans. Hilda C. Graef (New York: Paulist Press, 1954), 68-70.

11. Anthony de Mello, *The Song of the Bird* (New York: Doubleday, 1984), 21.

12. Ralph Waldo Emerson, "Experience," in *The Portable Emerson*, ed. Carl Bode (New York: Penguin, 1981), 269.

13. For Heidegger on the hand and thinking, see his "What Calls for Thinking?"; for Heidegger on "challenging-forth," see his "The Question concerning Technology," both in *Basic Writings*, ed. David Farrell Kress (San Francisco: Harper, 1993), 380-81 and 321-26, respectively.

14. Heidegger, "What Calls for Thinking?" 374-75.

15. Ralph Waldo Emerson, "Nature," in Bode, *The Portable Emerson*, 10-11.

16. Dillard, *Pilgrim at Tinker Creek*, 79.

17. Ibid., 80.

18. Ibid.

19. Ibid., 83.

20. Irenaeus, quoted in Leonardo Boff, *Sacraments of Life, Life of the Sacraments*, trans. John Drury (Beltsville, Md.: The Pastoral Press, 1987), 30.

21. Heidegger, "What Calls for Thinking?" 371.

22. Philip Hallie, *Lest Innocent Blood Be Shed* (New York: Harper Colophon, 1980), 68.

3. Beloved Community

1. Leonardo Boff, *Trinity and Society,* trans. Paul Burns (Maryknoll, N.Y.: Orbis Books, 1988), 108.

2. Sheila Durkin Dierks and Patricia Powers Ladley, *Catholic Worker Houses: Ordinary Miracles* (Kansas City, Mo.: Sheed & Ward, 1988), 86.

3. Dorothy Day, "On Pilgrimage," in *Dorothy Day: Selected Writings*, ed. Robert Ellsberg (Maryknoll, N.Y.: Orbis Books, 1992), 225.

4. For a good discussion of the West's general optimism about human nature, see John Passmore, *The Perfectibility of Man* (New York: Charles Scribner's Sons, 1970).

5. Sigmund Freud, *Civilization and Its Discontents*, trans. James Strachey (New York: W. W. Norton, 1989); Konrad Lorenz, *On Aggression*, trans. Marjorie K. Wilson (London: Methuen, 1966); Richard Dawkins, *The Selfish Gene* (New York: Oxford University Press, 1976).

6. Thomas Merton, *Asian Journal* (New York: New Directions, 1975), 307-8.

7. Although Nietzsche's discussions of the *ubermensch* are few and far between in his writings, they have attracted an incredible amount of attention. Interpretations of Nietzsche's comments range over a broad field. At one end are those commentators who read the *ubermensch* as a salutary spiritual or ethical ideal. At the other end are those who interpret it as a prototype of the Nazi Aryan conquerer. As I argue in the text, it is at least the prototype of rugged individualism. For Nietzsche's most extended discussion of the *ubermensch, see* "On the Higher Man" in Book 4 of *Thus Spoke Zarathustra*, in *The Portable Nietzsche*, ed. Walter Kaufmann (New York: Viking, 1968), 398-408.

8. Tom Wolfe's *The Bonfire of the Vanities* (New York: Bantam, 1988) takes the Nietzschean "blond beast" ideal to its logical conclusion,

showing just how painfully ludicrous it is. The Wall Street "masters of the universe" who are the novel's protagonists try to be kingdoms unto themselves, but their frenetic lifestyles—not to mention the unpredictability of high finance—give the lie to their illusions of security.

9. Jean-Paul Sartre claims this move is characteristic of ethnic prejudice (see *Anti-Semite and Jew*, trans. George J. Becker [New York: Schocken Books, 1995]).

10. Martin Luther King Jr., *Strength to Love* (Minneapolis, Minn.: Fortress Press), 91.

11. Boff, *Trinity and Society*, 4.

12. I've discussed the depersonalization of others at some length in *Practicing Presence: The Spirituality of Caring in Everyday Life* (Franklin, Wis.: Sheed & Ward, 2001).

13. Simone de Beauvoir, *Pyrrhus et Cineas* (Paris: Gallimard, 1944); idem, *The Ethics of Ambiguity*, trans. Bernard Frechtman (Secaucus, N.J.: Citadel, 1975). Thomas Merton makes a similar point in a 1961 letter to Dorothy Day. "To shut out the person and to refuse to consider him as a person [is to] block off the reality of the other. . . . We help ourselves to rise by helping him to rise. For when we extend our hand to the enemy who is sinking in the abyss, God reaches out to both of us, for it is He first of all who extends our hand to the enemy" (Thomas Merton, *The Hidden Ground of Love*, ed. William H. Shannon [New York: Harvest, 1985], 141).

14. For a good treatment of the early Christian community's understanding of hospitality, see Christine D. Polh, *Making Room: Recovering Hospitality as a Christian Tradition* (Grand Rapids, Mich.: Eerdmans, 1999).

15. Rosemary L. Haughton, "Hospitality: Home as the Integration of Privacy and Community," in *The Longing for Home*, ed. Leroy S. Rouner (Notre Dame, Ind.: University of Notre Dame Press, 1996), 212.

16. Henri Nouwen, *Reaching Out* (Garden City, N.Y.: Doubleday, 1975), 51.

17. Parker J. Palmer, *The Company of Strangers: Christianity and Renewal of America's Public Life* (New York: Crossroad, 1981), 68.

18. Martin Luther King Jr., *The Words of Martin Luther King, Jr.* (New York: Newmarket Press, 1981), 21.

19. Eberhard Arnold, *Why We Live in Community* (Framington, Pa.: Plough Publishing, 1995), 1.

20. Martin Luther King Jr., *Stride toward Freedom* (New York: Harper & Row, 1958), 88.

4. Taking the Downward Path

1. Noam Chomsky offers an even more chilling explanation of why the terrorist assaults so assaulted us. He claims that for the first time, the so-called Third World invaded the so-called First World, and that the unthinkability of this reversal of roles shook both the United States and Europe to their roots (Noam Chomsky, *9/11* [New York: Seven Stories Press, 2001], 12).

2. Dennis Smith's report from ground zero is a moving eyewitness record of the courageous attempts of rescue workers (Dennis Smith, *Ground Zero: The Story of the Rescue Efforts at the World Trade Center* [New York: Viking, 2002]).

3. Paul Johnson, "Relentlessly and Thoroughly: The Only Way to Respond," Lance Morrow, "The Case for Rage," and Daniel Lapin, "What the Face of Sheer Evil Looks Like," in *Beauty for Ashes: Spiritual Reflections on the Attack on America*, ed. John Farina (New York: Crossroad, 2002), 162, 153, 221.

4. William J. Bennett, *Why We Fight: Moral Clarity and the War on Terrorism* (New York: Doubleday, 2002).

5. Ibid., 16-17.

6. Ibid., 20.

7. Ibid., 33.

8. Henri Nouwen, *Here and Now: Living in the Spirit* (New York: Crossroad, 1994), 101.

9. Ibid., 100.

10. Ibid., 101.

11. Henri Nouwen, *The Path of Power* (New York: Crossroad, 1995), 8.

12. Henri Nouwen, *The Road to Daybreak: A Spiritual Journey* (New York: Doubleday, 1988), 154.

13. Henri Nouwen, *In the Name of Jesus: Reflections on Christian Leadership* (New York: Crossroad, 1989), 59.

14. Walter Wink, *Engaging the Powers* (Minneapolis, Minn.: Fortress Press, 1993), 141.

15. Thich Nhat Hanh, *Peace Is Every Step* (New York: Bantam, 1991), 96, 98.

16. Wink, *Engaging the Powers*, 217.

17. Rowan Williams, *Writing in the Dust: After September 11* (Grand Rapids, Mich.: Eerdmans, 2002), 6.

18. Ibid., 22-23, 24.